The Teachers' Lounge (Uncensored)

A Funny, Edgy, Poignant Look at Life in the Classroom

Kelly Flynn

ROWMAN & LITTLEFIELD EDUCATION
A division of
ROWMAN & LITTLEFIELD PUBLISHERS, INC.
Lanham • New York • Toronto • Plymouth, UK

Published by Rowman & Littlefield Education
A division of Rowman & Littlefield Publishers, Inc.
A wholly owned subsidary of The Rowman & Littlefield Publishing Group, Inc.
4501 Forbes Boulevard, Suite 200, Lanham, Maryland 20706
www.rowman.com

10 Thornbury Road, Plymouth PL6 7PP, United Kingdom

British Library Cataloguing in Publication Information Available

Library of Congress Cataloging-in-Publication Data

Library of Congress Cataloging-in-Publication Data Available
ISBN 978-1-4758-0032-6 (cloth : alk. paper) -- ISBN 978-1-4758-0033-3 (paper : alk. paper) --
ISBN 978-1-4758-0034-0 (electronic)

The paper used in this publication meets the minimum requirements of American National Standard for Information Sciences Permanence of Paper for Printed Library Materials, ANSI/NISO Z39.48-1992.

Printed in the United States of America

For the Teachers

If you teach a child to pass a test, he will learn for a day. If you teach a child to understand how he learns, he will learn for a lifetime.
—Kelly Flynn

IN PRAISE OF THE TEACHERS' LOUNGE (UNCENSORED)

"Every teacher should give a copy of this book to the mayor, to the school board, and to political representatives. It will astonish them and maybe increase their humility quotient. Written from inside classrooms, it is real. It is also fast-moving, funny, poignant, and occasionally shocking. Most important, the book is also hopeful, showing that whatever her successes and failures, every year, every class, every lesson, every student, the teacher comes back, certain she can do it better."
—**Susan Ohanian**, author of *What Happened to Recess and Why Are Our Children Struggling in Kindergarten?*

"Kelly Flynn is a powerhouse and must have been a great classroom teacher. I would have loved to work with her when I taught high school. Kelly always keeps her 'eyes on the prize,' the ability of teachers to influence the lives of their students. What is best about this book is that she is able to remain positive and hopeful about teaching despite all the difficulties of the job and the political and corporate assault on public schools, students, and especially teachers. I want to thank Kelly for reminding me why we chose to teach."
—**Alan Singer**, Hofstra University

"The media needs to spend time in the classroom and see what a teacher is up against today and tell that story without equivocation. This is what Kelly Flynn is writing about."
—**Frosty Troy**, founder and editor of *The Oklahoma Observer*

"With candor and humor, Kelly Flynn courageously tells the absurd-but-true stories from the public school classroom. Readers will come away understanding that teachers do what they do not for the merit pay or 'summers off,' but out of a profound sense of purpose, a commitment to education, and love."
—**Eileen Button**, author of *The Waiting Place: Learning to Appreciate Life's Little Delays*

Contents

Special Thanks

Heartfelt thanks to Nancy Carlsson-Paige for writing the Foreword for this book. Her expertise as a teacher educator and her strong sense of social justice make her a powerful advocate for teachers and the public school system. I am honored to include her voice in my book.

Thanks to Paul Keep, former editor of *The Flint Journal*, for his generous, open mind and for recognizing the fresh perspective a former teacher could bring to education coverage.

Thanks to my agent, Bertram Linder, for recognizing the broad appeal of this material and finding it a home. Thanks to Tom Koerner, my editor at Rowman & Littlefield Education, and to his assistant Carlie Wall, for guiding me through the publishing process.

"Just read it one more time, *pleeease,*" are words my husband, Norman Falconer, hears often, and he graciously drops whatever he is doing to read it, one more time. When Norman retired after thirty years in the classroom he was ready to leave the world of education behind. But he lets me drag him back, into every sort of philosophical discussion about teaching, learning, and the politics of education. Though he's happiest swinging a hammer he's an excellent wordsmith, too. I am infinitely grateful for his multi-talented brilliance, and for all the times he saved me from putting my foot squarely in my mouth.

Thanks to Kerry Flynn, my sister, my champion. In the way of sisters everywhere, we are wildly different, yet so much alike. What a blessing it is to move through this life knowing that someone so strong, smart, funny, and good-natured has my back. Thanks also to my creative, talented sister-in-law Denise Kabisch for the author photo for this book.

I'm grateful to my mom, Betty Flynn, who is as smart as she is beautiful. She told me from the beginning that I must have the courage to say the unpopular thing if it is a truth that needs to be said. I'm grateful to my dad, Dennis Flynn, for teaching me by example absolutely everything there is to know about optimism. I'm grateful to both of my parents for teaching me at an early age not to worry about other people's opinions of me. That lesson served me well as classroom teacher where a thick skin is essential, and ironically, as a newspaper columnist, too. It is truly a gift of freedom.

Deep and affectionate thanks to my friend and writing buddy, Eileen Button, author of *The Waiting Place.* The life of a writer is fraught with unique joys and piercing anxieties that only another writer truly understands. Her wisdom and humor have had a profound effect on my writing life in general, and on this book in particular.

If you were my student you were also my teacher, and I thank each and every one of you for providing me with infinite lessons in kindness and forgiveness in the school of human nature.

Thanks to Dr. Ann Trovillion-Timm, my high school writing teacher, for maintaining wicked high expectations. I use what I learned from her every day.

And, of course, sincere thanks to the teachers; to my own teachers, to my teaching colleagues, and to the teachers I affectionately call my "peeps," the ones who meet me in my virtual teachers' lounge and generously share their successes and frustrations about the murky world of teaching.

This book is dedicated to every teacher in every kind of classroom: large, small, rural, urban, suburban, public, private, charter. You are heroes, every day.

Most importantly, my deepest gratitude to the Universe, from whence all inspiration comes.

Foreword

Nancy Carlsson-Paige, Ed.D.

Things have gone very wrong with education policy in the U.S. in recent years, especially since the passage of the No Child Left Behind Act. There's too much testing in the schools, and an over-emphasis on accountability, all of which has led to a narrowing of the curriculum at all levels of schooling, a loss of the arts, recess, and other nontested subjects, and more didactic instruction. Kelly Flynn's book, rich with essays about real schools—about teachers, students, and the issues they live with—reminds us of what we have lost sight of in recent years: schools are for learning academic skills, but they are also places where we learn to live together in a human community.

In the current education climate, teachers get blamed for kids' low test scores, and for the persistent gap in performance between low-income and black and Hispanic students and their peers. Kelly Flynn was a teacher for many years. She knows from experience how hard teachers work, how they will go to bat for a kid in need, how they put in the extra hours and effort without complaining. She understands that it's easier to blame teachers for school failings than to face or do anything about the underlying causes of the achievement gap.

The achievement gap exists before children ever meet their teachers. It's caused by social forces that exist outside of the classroom—by poverty and inequality.

These are words we hear too rarely today. They're words that have been replaced by other words: standardized tests, accountability, failing schools, merit pay, Race to the Top—words that portray education as a competition instead of the deeply human, relational, cooperative activity that it is. Words that imply that only some children and schools—the ones who perform as mandated—deserve to get to the top.

The essays in *The Teachers' Lounge (Uncensored)* remind us of the day-to-day human interactions that go on inside the walls of a school—the messy dynamics among teachers, kids, administrators, and parents. We realize that in schools children learn to help one another, learn to be part of a group, and that teachers collaborate. We understand that the business values of competition and measurement that are imposed on today's schools are all wrong for this vibrant place.

Teachers cannot thrive in environments where they are measured, compared, and threatened. Children can't learn in these environments either. You can drill kids and get their test scores up. You can take away recess and field trips, the arts and activity based learning to make time for more test prep. But real learning is not rote learning. Real learning is thinking in original ways, knowing how to apply ideas, growing morally as well as intellectually.

Ultimately, Kelly Flynn offers us a hopeful message. She understands that we have the national resources to support a successful education system. She knows that one of our greatest resources is teachers. And she tells us that you and I have the power to insist on more for our kids. We all deserve an education system that gives every kid a fair and equal chance and not just a lottery ticket to vie for a spot in a coveted charter school. We need an education system that is funded centrally and equally, where additional resources go to the poorest districts.

When we see an end to teacher bashing, high stakes tests, and resources for some but not all, when we create a just and equitable education system for our nation's children, then schools will be places where every child wants to be and can find success. These will be schools where living and learning are not separate. They'll be schools where kids achieve not only academically, but also where they learn to build community, to appreciate diversity, and to resolve conflicts nonviolently. The society of the future will need citizens who have such skills—citizens who can think for themselves, feel compassion for others, and stand up for what is right.

■■■

Nancy Carlsson-Paige is Professor Emerita at Lesley University where she taught teachers for more than 30 years and was a founder of the University's Center for Peaceable Schools. A strong advocate for public education, Nancy works with other education activists for the rights of all children to a quality education. Nancy has authored five books and numerous articles and op eds. She is an advocate for education that promotes social justice and the well being of all children.

Preface

It was second hour and we were in lock-down mode. "Lock-down" was a term we became uneasily familiar with in the post-Columbine era. It meant that teachers and students were locked into their classrooms because some sort of threat had been made against the school or someone in it.

We, of course, had no idea what that threat was. We just knew that no one could enter or leave our classrooms, even to go to the bathroom, until we got the all-clear signal. The fact that we couldn't leave meant that immediately every student wanted to, desperately. We all felt anxious, restless, and trapped.

I was simply relieved that it was second hour. If I had to be trapped with any group of kids, I was glad it was this one. As is typical in scheduling, the luck of the draw results in some classes that purr like well-oiled machines, and others that stall, sputter, and groan like rusty old jalopies. This particular group of freshmen was collectively more mature than most: polite, smart, and fun to be with.

But they didn't have to be gifted to see the flaws in this plan.

"Ms. Flynn," said Brian, rapidly tapping two pencils on his desk to some internal beat. "What good is a locked door when we have all those windows?" He jerked his head in the direction of the wall of windows, also locked. "If someone wants in, they'll just break the glass."

"Yeah," said Andrea. "And besides, if someone in the hall has a gun they can just shoot off the doorknob. This is really dumb."

For the next half hour the kids, who had been practically raised by the television set and weaned on crime TV, matter-of-factly discussed every possible scenario. They weren't afraid, merely bored.

What could I say? It did seem dumb. The plan was full of holes and everyone in that building knew it. Still, what was the alternative? To do nothing? Or to build schools that resembled prisons, places that kids dreaded coming to even more than they already did?

As I sat with my second-hour students, my eyes flitting from the door to the window to the clock, and as second hour dragged slowly into third, I thought about how the general public doesn't really "get" the public school experience today. Sure, there would be a short, dry news story about the incident in the paper, but it wouldn't come close to describing how we felt, held captive in that room, wondering what the heck was going on, half listening for gunshots or explosions.

And that's one of the biggest problems facing education today, that disconnect between what *really* goes on in schools, and what policy makers and the general public *think* goes on in schools.

Every single day in the classroom teachers and students meet dozens of challenges that interfere with teaching and learning. Some of these challenges seem almost silly, like dress codes, Kleenex shortages, and messy backpacks. Others are huge and daunting, like bomb threats, poverty, and drug abuse.

Current education legislation and reform efforts ignore all of that. Instead, they point with laser-like focus to standardized tests as the be-all and end-all of education. And as legislators move American education steadily toward more data-driven reforms, anecdotal evidence is lost in the chalk dust.

But it is our stories, rich with the culture of our life and times that reveal what kind of help educators really need to improve the learning environment for students. Anecdotal evidence is every bit as valuable as data—perhaps even more so—precisely because it describes things that cannot be measured, yet have a profound effect on teaching and learning.

We can't "reform" education until we see it clearly. But we will never see it clearly if we insist on defining students and their teachers by test scores.

We have to look at the big picture.

When I left the classroom after twenty years of teaching I began telling these stories. Drawing from the teaching journal that I kept to vent my frustration at the absurdity of the mandates that were handed down to classroom teachers, I wrote a weekly newspaper column about education from a teacher's point of view. For seven years the column ran on the Sunday opinion page of *The Flint Journal* and in the *Jackson Citizen Patriot*.

These stories celebrate every messy detail of teaching and learning and life in the classroom. As Nancy Carlsson-Paige noted in the Foreword, "...schools are for learning academic skills, but they are also places where we learn to live together in a human community." She describes education as a "deeply human, relational, cooperative activity."

I couldn't agree more.

The chapter titles of this book, Teachers, Students, Parents, Community, and Policy, reflect the key elements that shape that human community. My intention is to give you a peek inside the walls of a typical public high school. Chances are you won't hear this point of view from the people you know who are actually working in schools, because if there is one thing educators are afraid of, it's that they'll say the wrong thing and be perceived as unprofessional. So they spout the party line and make nice, zealously guarding the truth and the reputations of their schools.

And the truth is this: This thing called education is complicated, messy, difficult, humbling, aggravating beyond belief, and fleetingly, deeply rewarding.

This is a side of the story that is never told. Almost all education coverage in the mainstream media is told from an outsider looking in.

I tell the story from the inside looking out.

Chapter One

Teachers

From first impressions and second chances to nuked fish and being punked

A teacher affects eternity; he can never tell where his influence stops.
—Henry Adams

A WING AND A PRAYER

Of course there's prayer in school.

Ms. Gilbert prayed every single day before third hour.

Fervently.

Because sometimes, luck of the draw in scheduling stacks classes with an assortment of students so disinterested in learning that one wonders why they bother to show up at all.

Every teacher experiences it. For Ms. Gilbert, this science class was a challenge from the first day in September to the last day in June.

The scene never varied: the girls with their makeup, mirrors held high, inspecting their pores, adding yet more eye liner where there's already too much, an arsenal of beauty products spread across their desks where schoolbooks should be.

Those girls chattering furiously, and—sorry—stupidly, about some boy who cheated on a friend, electrified by the juicy details of that morning's confrontation. Unwillingly, the mind fast-forwards to the same girls as women, still obsessed with trashy gossip, the setting a bar instead of a classroom. Already their faces are settling into hard lines in hard makeup. They don't take kindly to having to shelve this titillating talk until class is over.

The boys are quiet, but it's a quiet born of apathy rather than good behavior. They sit and stare, dazed, eyes glazed, mouths open, not daydreaming exactly, but drugged looking and unresponsive, indifferent, withdrawn.

One boy shuffles in with pants hung low, empty hands shoved deep into the pockets of a dirty hoodie. No backpack, no textbook, no paper, no pencil—no pretext of learning at all. He slouches into his seat, drops his head, and flops his hood over his face. Less than a minute later drool puddles on his desk.

Ms. Gilbert gazes at her class and not one single student appears to have come to learn. As proof of this the tardy bell rings and the kids continue unfazed, talking, laughing, gossiping, sleeping, staring. The bell is meaningless to them.

There's no doubt about it. A class like this can wither the spirits of the best teacher. If you let them, teenagers will make you feel incidental, irrelevant, insignificant. You're a nuisance, an interloper, an imposition. It takes an incredible strength of will to stand up to that every day.

Really, truly, she doesn't know whether to laugh or to cry. This group is so unfocused, so *not* ready to learn, that she wants to put her own head down on her desk.

But she doesn't. She says a silent amen, takes a deep breath, and moves forward, walking between the rows. A tap on a desk here, a murmur there, whispering names, making eye contact, connecting.

"Okay," she says. "Let's begin . . ."

BEHIND THE WALLS

"I don't have a pencil!"
   "I lost my book!"
   "This class is boring!"
   "This school sucks!"

Those who currently drive education policy in this country have no idea how often teachers hear such sentiments each day. The clientele has changed dramatically since the days when chewing gum in class was a discipline issue of consequence. That's not to say that kids are "bad." They're not. Teachers generally enjoy their students and work hard to connect with them. But as society and our culture evolve, the kids and what parents expect from them has evolved, too, and all of that plays out in classrooms in wildly diverse ways.

Make no mistake—a lot of excellent teaching and learning happens in thousands of classrooms every day. But it would be disingenuous not to acknowledge that it's getting harder due to changing dynamics in the public school system. To imagine that all kids sit attentively in their seats, ready and eager to learn, is to imagine that the bluebird of happiness stops by for lunch, too.

Kids want hands-on experience, but they get test-prep and drill. They want to learn at their own pace, but they get scripted lessons with a strict timeline. They want to learn things that are relevant to their lives, but they get the Common Core Standards. They want teachers who truly see them in all of their unique glory, but they get force-fed a one-size-fits-all education.

The problem with most education policy is that it's being created by people who have never taught school. In fact in most cases, the key players leading education reform have spent almost no time in a classroom since they were students themselves.

Before we get started here, let's take a look at the key players:

Teenagers: They are simultaneously the most charming and the most exasperating people on the planet. One minute they hide behind a flat-eyed, curled-lip insolence that could stop a Navy Seal in his tracks. The next minute their innocence, vulnerability and kindness will bring you to tears.

Administrators: Some have your back, but for others, Alzheimer's runs rampant. The minute they become administrators most forget what it was like to be a classroom teacher. Worse yet, some were hired as administrators without any classroom experience at all.

Teachers: Brave, tenacious and world-weary, they struggle to teach the required curriculum while wearing several hats at once: disciplinarian, parent, social worker, counselor, psychologist, referee. No one in America is lied to more often except cops and Senate investigating committees.

Parents: These are the real power players in the equation. When it comes to public education what parents want, parents get. They are the customers, and the customer is always right. This can be a fine thing, for example, when they rally support for a failing band program. But it's a bad, bad thing when one parent can undermine a school discipline policy.

School Board: This is a mixed breed, a cross between politicians and administrators. At best they have some knowledge of the learning process. At worst, they operate purely from ego to satisfy a personal power trip or political aspiration.

Politicians: They shamelessly use education as a bargaining chip in their game of politics. They hold the purse strings and give lip service to education, but rarely make a positive difference in day-to-day teaching and learning. That they sell out children to corporate interests should be punishable by law.

So this is it. The nitty-gritty, down-and-dirty side of public education.

It's not for the faint of heart.

ONE OF OUR OWN

People make assumptions when they find out that you're a teacher. They start acting funny, self-consciously, the way they might around a nun or a minister.

For one thing, they immediately assume that teachers are goody-two-shoes. They apologize for swearing in front of teachers, as if they're afraid they might get sent to the principal's office. They wait until you've left the room to tell the latest dirty joke. And they always pull a teacher aside to share their own school woes, their personal learning difficulties, the teachers they loved, and the teachers they hated.

But like animals in the wild, teachers always recognize one of their own. In any venue where a group of teachers might gather, such as a restaurant or a pub, teachers can spot their own kind in a heartbeat.

And it's not just the sensible shoes, wash-and-wear wardrobe, or wholesome openness that make teachers so easy to spot. It's an aura of authority that follows teachers, even after they've retired. It's the sense of control, the feeling that if a fire breaks out, they'll be the first out of their seats, forming lines and directing people out of the burning building.

Of necessity teachers are keen observers, aware of their surroundings, alert to the collective mood, tuned in to the noise around them. But they're conscious of being observed, too. They're held to a higher standard and they know it. Most every teacher has been blind-sided by an angry parent and no matter how unfair the allegation, how far-fetched the story or how rude the insult, they're more likely than not to listen and respond calmly.

They're constantly conscious of the example they set for students, the scrutiny they face from parents, and the image they portray to the media. It colors every decision they make, every word they utter. They are acutely aware of their position as role model. They know that the way they handle themselves is watched not only by parents, administrators, and the community, but most importantly, by their students.

Crowd control is second nature, too, turning trips to busy malls into tests in self-restraint. When they come across groups of people standing and chatting in the middle of the aisle it takes every ounce of self-restraint not to bellow, "Move along people! Don't block the road, please!"

That sense of authority spills into all areas of their lives, not just the classroom. Thus, teachers have no qualms about telling kids to behave—even when they belong to somebody else.

Take for instance, Mr. Conroy, a twenty-five-year history teacher with a good sense of humor but no tolerance for misbehavior. One day while pushing his cart through the grocery store, he hears a little boy arguing loudly with his mother three aisles away. Mom has no control and the boy is being a brat, grabbing cereal boxes off the shelves and tossing them on the floor. The commotion is astounding. The boy escapes and comes skipping down Mr. Conroy's aisle, sliding to a stop in front of him.

Without missing a beat Mr. Conroy points a finger at the boy and barks, "HEY! You mind your mother!" The boy's eyes nearly pop out of his head in surprise and he turns on his heel and runs. All is quiet after that.

Another time Mr. Conroy and his wife went to see *Titanic* at a local movie theater. Five minutes into the movie, four kids arrived, thirteen to fourteen years old. They proceeded to laugh and talk loudly, stand up, change seats, and kick the seats of the people in front of them. Annoyed, people grumbled and shot them dirty looks. Just as Mr. Conroy was about to get up and go over, a man a few seats away turned around and pinpointed the kids with a look. "Excuse me," he said sternly. "We expect to enjoy this movie in peace. Sit down and don't make another sound." The startled kids sat down. They didn't make another sound.

On the way out of the theater Mr. Conroy found himself walking next to the man. Giving the man a friendly nudge with his elbow he raised his eyebrows inquiringly.

"Teacher?" Mr. Conroy asked.

"Yeah," the man sighed.

Mr. Conroy nodded in understanding.

WHERE'S MY CAPE?

Sometimes teachers hear the most amazing things in their classrooms:

"Hey, Steve, I heard you had another party this weekend."

"Yeah, man, I did. My parents were out of town again. It was great!"

"Dude, how do you get away with it? You have more parties than anyone I know. Don't your neighbors tell your parents?"

"Oh, no, man, 'cause I use the signs."

"The signs? What signs?"

"You know, the birthday signs. I made these big signs, you know, like you make for someone's birthday, poster board stapled to a stick. I use bright colored markers and make the letters all fancy, then I stick the sign in the ground in my yard on the day of the party. In between, I keep the signs under my mattress so my mom doesn't find them."

"Well, what do the signs say?"

"This week it said, 'Happy 50th Birthday Aunt Bertha!' See, the neighbors think it's a family party for some old lady. It's genius, man!"

Sometimes it's a blessing, and sometimes it's a curse, but there's no escaping the Super Powers.

That's right. Super Powers. Years of hearing and seeing it all have honed teachers' senses and instincts to super-hero levels.

Supersonic hearing is just one of the Super Powers. Teachers can also spot the same answer on two student's papers, even if they're from a different hour and are graded several hours apart. They can tell by the handwriting whether a paper belongs to a boy or a girl, and usually know exactly which of their 130 students it belongs to. Super elastic bladders allow them to go six hours without a bathroom break. And they can spot a lie almost before it's uttered.

During a test they know which kid is asking his neighbor for a pencil, and which one is asking for an answer. They know when a kid really has to use the bathroom and when he just wants to go for a walk. They know when a kid doesn't understand something, even if he says he does. And all the little hairs on the backs of their necks stand up when a fight is about to break out.

Mr. Bryson, a tenth grade English teacher known for his Mark Twain impersonations, hurries down the hall on his way to the office. Ricky Warchawski is standing in front of his locker with six girls clustered around him. Ricky is a bigger-than-life character, not only in size, but in spirit and enthusiasm and energy. Loud. Playful. Kind. He's one of those rare kids who is part of no clique, but welcome in all, easily crossing social lines because of his open, good heart.

Mr. Bryson has exactly five minutes to get to the office and back before the bell rings. He's moving fast.

As he approaches Ricky, Mr. Bryson sees that the boy is holding something carefully in his hand. At about five feet away he realizes that it is a clear plastic baggie. And there is something in it.

Something moving.

He's really hustling, so he doesn't slow down.

"Whatcha' got in the bag, Ricky?" he asks.

"Crickets!" Ricky booms. "Want one?!" And grinning from ear to ear he takes a cricket out of the bag and holds it out to Mr. Bryson. (Why does he have a baggie full of crickets? Sometimes, you just don't ask.)

"No, thanks, not today," Mr. Bryson says, smiling. As he passes the group of kids, Ricky turns to the girls and waves the cricket in their faces, laughing at their squeals.

Mr. Bryson sails on by. Without looking back or breaking stride he says over his shoulder, "And take it out of your mouth, please."

Full blown screams.

"Eewwww! How did you know he was going to *do* that?!" the girls cry. Mr. Bryson glances back just in time to see Ricky pull the cricket out of his mouth.

Yep, it's true. They have eyes in the backs of their heads, too.

TRIAL BY FIRE

There can't be a job on earth as hard as the first year of teaching. It's an initiation by fire, a marathon sprint to June, with no let-up and not a moment for contemplation or reflection.

Self-doubt. Frustration. Exhaustion. Meet your new best friends.

Consider the plight of Ms. Mitchell, a recent Michigan State University graduate who survived the year from hell. It was so bad, in fact, that it's hard to believe she ever went back.

Initially, Ms. Mitchell is assigned five sections of freshman English. Not bad, she thinks. She can focus on one thing and get really good at it.

Meanwhile, Mr. Stoddard, a stern man with twenty-five years of experience, complains mightily to administrators about the injustice of a first-year teacher getting a cushy one-prep schedule. Twenty-four hours later he has her schedule and she has his: Eighth Grade Reading Lab, Ninth Grade Reading Lab, Writing Lab and Yearbook. She is a brand new teacher with four preps that include a student publication.

The Reading and Writing Labs are full of poor readers and low achievers, including nineteen special education students, even more than the special ed teachers are allowed to have on their caseloads.

When she walks into her classroom the first day, young Ms. Mitchell is completely unprepared for the cold stares of tough-looking kids. They sit with arms crossed over chests and glare. She is terrified.

But wait. It gets worse.

A new computer-based reading program is being piloted down the street at the regional educational service agency and the superintendent decrees that her school will participate. Three hours of instruction later, she is put in charge.

Her days become one long race against the clock. She arrives at school at 6:30 in the morning to get some uninterrupted work done. She teaches first hour in her classroom, then boards a school bus with her second hour students for a five-minute trip down the road to the service agency to spend forty minutes on the computers. They rush back onto the bus, back to the school, and she teaches an hour in her classroom.

Yearbook class includes a $20,000 contract with a company that requires her to create, publish, sell and distribute 800 copies of a book.

Then it's back to the bus with another class, back to the service agency, race through another lesson, and back to the bus in time to meet sixth hour in her classroom.

To top it all off, there is record rainfall that season and she spends part of each day standing in it, taking roll as her students get on and off the bus. She is terrified that she will lose one along the way.

It is grueling. Sheer stubbornness keeps her going.

She also experiences her first really mean, possibly unstable parent, Mrs. Blackstone. Trina Blackstone is a nice girl and Ms. Mitchell has no problems with her. But like all bullies, Trina's mother has decided to focus her misplaced anger on the most vulnerable, in this case, the newest teacher on staff. In phone call after phone call Mrs. Blackstone issues orders and ultimatums. First, she orders Ms. Mitchell to move her daughter's seat. Trina seems to be doing fine where she is, but Ms. Mitchell complies. The next day Mrs. Blackstone calls as if she never issued that order, and angrily demands to know why Ms. Mitchell moved her daughter's seat. Another day, Ms. Mitchell compliments Trina on an assignment in front of the class. The next day she gets a call from Mrs. Blackstone angrily accusing her of embarrassing Trina.

It's like tip-toeing through land mines.

On and on it goes, Mrs. Blackstone's emotional rollercoaster holding Ms. Mitchell hostage. For an entire year she fields calls from Mrs. Blackstone, doing her best to be professional, but secretly worrying that the woman might somehow get her fired. The absurdity of her yo-yoing demands might even be funny if it weren't all so darn serious.

Ms. Mitchell feels old overnight. While her friends are having fun in their first jobs and going out to play at the end of the day, she trudges out of the building each night carrying a heavy cloth bag full of papers to grade, taking her work home with her both literally and figuratively. She feels weighted down with responsibility, accountability. Evenings and weekends are spent preparing lessons and grading papers, frantically trying to stay one step ahead of the kids. The low salary does not bother her. She doesn't have time to spend it, anyway.

Not a single thing she learned in college prepared her for that first year. And she learned more that first year on the job than she did in four years of college. The thing that she most desperately needs, techniques for classroom management and discipline, are far hairier in actual practice with real kids than as theories in a textbook.

Like some sort of screwy boot camp, the first year tests her stamina, her professionalism, her psychological stability, and her dedication.

So why does she go back?

She goes back because she's sure she can do better. Every year, every class, every lesson, every student, she's certain she can do it better.

Teachers face a lot of failure in the classroom. Their students'. And their own.

But right around every corner, there's another opportunity to succeed.

COLLEGE DIDN'T TEACH THIS

When rookie teachers step to the front of that classroom for the very first time, shoes shined, pencils sharpened, and perfectly typed handouts hot off the Xerox machine, it can be a swift sharp blow to the ego if students don't respond the way the rookie imagined they would.

Armed with a change-the-world attitude and a lovingly prepared lesson plan the rookie teacher enthusiastically begins, only to come to a confused stop when she realizes. . . they're not listening.

Whisperwhisperwhisperwhisper.

What in the world? The rookie looks around in surprise.

Whisperwhisperwhisperwhisper.

She stops and waits, pinpointing the whisperers with a hard look. They quiet down.

She smiles and continues.

Whisperwhisperwhisperwhisper.

She stops again, completely unnerved. Of all the things she thought might go wrong today—losing the key to her classroom, forgetting her grade book, inadvertently leaving out part of the lesson, wearing two different colored socks—it never once occurred to her that the students wouldn't listen.

And she can't imagine why they aren't. This stuff is interesting. Useful. They need it and if they just give it a chance, they will love it. She's as certain of the relevance of this material as she is of her own name. So why aren't they listening? Why aren't they hanging on every word of this fabulous lesson?

And more importantly, *why hadn't anyone warned her about this?!*

Well, eventually, through trial and error, she does learn techniques for getting students' attention and making them listen (or at least be quiet while she talks). But unfortunately, that is just the first of many Things No One Told Her about teaching. Other rude awakenings include:

No one told her that she would be transformed overnight from a fun-loving college coed to a world-weary fuddy-duddy who (gladly) goes to bed at 8:30 every night. One day she is a life-of-the-party kind of girl, and the next she drops wearily into a chair in the teachers' lounge and wails, "What happened to me? I used to be *fun!*"

No one told her that when it comes to the copy machine, it's every woman for herself. Even when she arrives at 6:30 in the morning she has to stand in line. They also didn't tell her that she'd spend half her time at said copy machine on her hands and knees with her fanny in the air, trying not to get black gunk on her clothes while she tries in vain to get it un-jammed.

No one told her how dirty schools are, that she would eventually give up her professional suits for a wash-and-wear wardrobe. That she would trade in her heels for flats so that she can sprint down the hall in pursuit of the kids who ignore her requests to remove their hats or throw away their soft drinks.

No one told her that she was entering a profession where the biggest perk would be a plastic chip-clip or refrigerator magnet, given to her by her teaching association on National Teacher Day.

No one told her that she would need to grow a reptilian-thick skin to protect herself from the sheer meanness of teenagers, their parents, and the public.

No one told her that feelings of helplessness and heartbreak would sometimes overwhelm her when she witnessed the poor, neglectful, abusive home lives of some of her students.

No one told her that some of these kids aren't kids at all, but rather hardened criminals who don't belong in a school with real kids.

Everyone talks about summers off. But no one told her that she was entering a profession that would suck the very life-blood out of her if she let it. No one told her that no matter how much she does it will never be enough. That when she is done for the day, in addition to the stacks of papers she has to grade, there will be meetings upon meetings upon meetings to attend, kids to tutor, teams to coach, dances to chaperone, clubs to sponsor and theater performances to attend. That administrators would demand more, parents would demand more, students would demand more. No one told her that when she signed on with a school district she might as well keep food in her desk and a change of clothes in her cabinet, because she's never going home again.

THE ESSENCE OF TEACHING AND LEARNING

Did you get the good teacher?!

That's the burning question among students and parents when the start of school draws near. Anxious and eager, parents and students haunt the mailbox for those notification letters, hoping to learn that their teacher requests were honored.

Truly savvy parents make wise choices based on their child's learning style and the instructor's teaching style. But more often than not the choice is less informed. Parents swap stories and word-of-mouth—including every sort of exaggeration—travels fast.

It's a dilemma that school districts across the country struggle with; how do you fairly distribute kids among teachers when so many parents make specific requests?

And though the government's narrow notion of good teaching has changed in recent years with the "highly qualified" portion of the No Child

Left Behind Act, in reality, the recipe for quality teaching has not changed at all.

Ideally, the recipe would have two ingredients: a teacher with a passion for his subject, and students who love to learn. When those two ingredients are present, the result is the essence of teaching and learning, where success is the only possible solution because the participants make it easy for each other. It's called the "teachable moment," that moment when Jupiter aligns with Mars, everything falls into place, teachers teach and kids learn, effortlessly. It's that zing that happens when the ball hits the sweet spot on a tennis racket.

It's as exhilarating as a runner's high and makes teachers feel as though they could teach forever. And it's why they became teachers in the first place, the thrill of teaching something they love to someone who is eager to learn it.

But too often it feels as though their running shoes are filled with lead because kids come to the equation with so many problems: mental, physical, emotional abuse. Parents who don't value education. Poverty. Substance abuse, either by the parents, the student, or both. Mental illness. Physical illness. Criminal records. Kids who come from homes that have no reading material whatsoever.

Teachers often wade through muck so deep that they are thrilled simply to get every student on task, let alone to hit that stride where the teaching and learning happens effortlessly and the participants make it easy for each other. And that's what eventually smothers the fire, that sense of having to do so many things that you can't do any of them well.

A tattered news clipping dated November 29, 1950, from the *Owosso Argus Press* reported that the PTA of Byron schools in Michigan discussed the qualities of a good teacher. The consensus was that a good teacher enjoys teaching, likes kids, and knows his subject matter. They decided that a sense of humor helped, too.

So little has changed.

Well over half a century later, parental consensus is the same; they want teachers who love their kids, and know their stuff.

Byron PTA members went on to warn parents that their attitude toward teachers in the home would be reflected in the child's attitude toward teachers in the classroom.

That hasn't changed, either. A parent's insistence on a certain teacher may very well send the wrong message about teachers in general.

Bottom line, if the child is fairly well adjusted, it's probably best to leave the teacher assignment up to chance. After all, this is but one in a long line of teachers. Teaching a child to adapt and flourish in new situations with a variety of teaching styles, may ultimately prove to be more valuable than getting the teacher of choice.

Consider this quote from *We Took to the Woods* by Louise Dickinson Rich: "The excellence of a teacher has nothing at all to do with his background, or the amount of salary he is paid, or anything else except his own personality and inherent bent. A good teacher is born, I am convinced, and his presence would make a good school out of a woodshed."

The copyright of that book is 1942.

As schools struggle to be accommodating, yet fair, with classroom assignments, think about this: There's a very good chance that it has crossed more than one teacher's mind how truly lovely it might be to hand pick their students.

But they don't. They embrace them all.

TO TEACH, WITH LOVE

Old habits die hard.

Which is why Ms. Gilbert found herself in front of the DVD player on Labor Day, watching the 1967 film *To Sir, With Love* for the eighteenth time. As part of her annual back-to-school ritual she watched this movie, year after year, in search of the answer to that most perplexing question: How do teachers make students like and respect them, without simply giving in to their demands?

Because that's what it takes to be a truly great teacher. The kids need to like and respect you. Even the most difficult kid will try for a teacher he likes, and a good student can be turned off by a teacher he doesn't.

Though it's set in the 1960s the story is timeless. Mouthy, insolent, yet compelling teens test a new teacher, almost to the breaking point. The very human teacher has a eureka moment, takes back control of his classroom, and eventually wins their respect, and their hearts.

The story is timeless because human nature doesn't change. Trends in education come and go, legislation changes and technology advances, but learning almost always boils down to the relationship between the student and the teacher.

A gifted teacher can teach a child to read using a stick in the dirt and the backyard as his classroom. But an antagonistic teacher can have every possible resource at his disposal, and still never reach a child.

At the end of the movie Lulu sings the theme song, the students present Thackeray (Sidney Poitier) with a gift, he changes his mind and decides to stay in education after all, and once again Ms. Gilbert reaches for the Kleenex.

In reality, though, such crystallizing moments for teachers are few and far between. Oh, they have lots of one-on-one successes, poignant moments when they really connect with a student. But rarely are kids organized enough to make cinematic drama.

Just before he retired, though, Mr. Falconer was lucky enough to experience an almost-movie moment. He taught Advanced Placement (AP) history to sophomores. The classes were small, the students smart, spirited, motivated, and curious.

One year his AP History group was particularly fun and engaged. A student named Maria started every single session by dropping into her seat and asking enthusiastically, "So, what are we going to learn today, Teach?" It was one of those rare groups where everyone clicked and the chemistry hummed. It was a teacher's dream come true.

Fast forward two years, and the students from that class are now seniors and, as is the tradition at their school, are sprung from high school a week before the rest of the student body. It's a hot June day, and Mr. Falconer is teaching his current AP class of sophomores.

Suddenly the door opens. Silently, the entire AP class from two years before files into the room and sits down.

The sophomores gape, awed by the upperclassmen.

"So, what are we going to learn today, Teach?" Maria asks.

And though their time as students in that school was over, those seniors stayed, all hour, to listen to his lesson.

Pass the Kleenex, please.

BULLIED

"I've always wanted to work with kids."

"I want to inspire students."

"I can make a difference."

Ask a teacher why they chose education, and often they'll say they've felt the call to teach their entire lives.

At some point, though, most come to the realization that the reality of the classroom is not quite as enchanting as they envisioned. It's not easy. It's not all sweetness and light. And a lot of kids don't care about learning.

That's okay. Teachers adjust. At least, most of them do.

Some don't though. Some spend their careers in a fierce struggle that they can't name, but that they know they're losing.

They become The Bullied Teacher.

The issue of bullying among students—especially cyber bullying—is big news. Almost every state has passed some sort of antibullying legislation.

But what is just as sad, just as ugly, and yet almost never discussed, is the plight of the bullied teacher.

Mr. Crichton has been the bullied teacher since he started teaching in 1992. What he lacks in stature he makes up for in sincerity. He has warm brown eyes, a ready smile, and is infinitely kind. He doesn't have the capacity for anger. His gentle temperament should be an asset in the classroom, but it's not.

The kids walk all over him.

Students read his kindness as wimpiness. His size makes him appear weak. To the students, his beat-up shoes, corduroy pants and ill-fitting shirts spell "dork."

If a student bothered to get to know him, they would have an advocate for life. In him they would find their biggest cheerleader, most loyal supporter, and wisest counsel.

But they don't. They throw spitwads at the chalkboard, mock his overbite behind his back, and make squeaky mouse noises while he talks.

They do not listen to him. They are sure he has nothing worthwhile to say.

The thing is, it never seems to deter him. He still approaches every student with a great big open heart.

And an open textbook. Science delights him and when a student does venture to ask a question, he answers it clearly, succinctly, and oh, so earnestly. But the fact that he lights up when talking about photosynthesis and ecosystems only fuels their disdain.

Sometimes, after a tough first year bullied teachers get their bearings, get some help, and make changes that work.

But some don't. They may, on some level, know they aren't connecting, but don't know exactly why. They also don't recognize themselves as bullied. And if they do, they find it awfully hard to give up their dream of working with kids.

Mr. Crichton had so much knowledge to share, so much goodness in his heart.

With less predatory students, he could have thrived.

STINK HAVEN

There's something mysterious in the public school system that students never see and people know little about. Deep secrets hide there and great and small discussions happen there. It is a place of hushed voices and robust laughter.

It's the teachers' lounge.

Most people think the lounge is for grading papers and writing lesson plans, but to teachers, it's much, much more.

Part haven and part asylum, reeking of stinky feet and old soup, it's a place where teachers can kick off their shoes and sit for a moment. It's a place to grab a bad cup of coffee from a dirty pot, or a cold can of pop from a temperamental machine, though chances are they won't have time to finish either.

Student teachers are cautioned by professors to stay out of the lounge, fearing that negativity is contagious. And in a job where you spend most of your time trying to make kids do something they don't want to do, there is plenty of that. But it's also a place where a rookie can learn from experienced teachers what they weren't taught in college: the subtleties of classroom management and student discipline.

To call it a lounge is a bit of a stretch. Little free time leaves little time for lounging, and most aren't conducive to lounging anyway. As student populations grow in buildings too small, every available space is needed for instruction. So the lounge is usually an afterthought, sporting beat-up, cast-off furniture and tables sticky with yesterday's lunch. Noisy old refrigerators full of furry, forgotten food sit next to ancient microwaves, interiors thick with splattered food and smells—*"my God, who nuked the leftover fish?!"*

From somebody's garden surplus to batches of burned cookies, food left in the lounge is snatched and snarfed quickly. Nothing is too old or too gross.

Mice are frequent visitors, though principals are not, conversation tending to stop when they enter. But gripes aired in the lounge make their way to administrators anyway. Not because the lounge is bugged (except for ants and roaches), but because every school has a mole, sucking up to the brass.

A timid knock signals a student at the door and teachers wait each other out to see who will answer it. But shouts and hollers from outside have teachers dropping sandwiches and springing from seats to break up a fight in the hall.

It's a marketplace for trading classroom materials, selling homemade crafts, and hawking a daughter's Girl Scout cookies. And come November, instead of a football pool, teachers buy squares betting on the date of the first snow day.

One person in the wrong chair throws everyone for a loop, disrupting the imaginary seating chart established the first few days of school.

Academic arguments last forever; does a comma go before "and" in a series? Teachers of business and English disagree.

In the sanctuary of the teachers' lounge, tempers flare and success is celebrated. Teachers cry, and sometimes laugh 'til they cry.

But one thing is certain; just a few minutes reprieve from students can make all the difference in the world.

A TEACHER'S CRIME

There's no glee in this secret. There's no thrill in the hearing, or in the telling of it. In fact, this secret brings such a flood of conflicting emotions that teachers are at once met with a need to talk about it, and an unwillingness to voice it aloud.

It's the sickening feeling that teachers get upon learning that one of their colleagues has been accused of sexual impropriety.

First, disbelief: How could someone they ate lunch with and shared lesson plans with and stood in line for the copy machine with, possibly be guilty of something like. . .that? Wouldn't they have suspected? Wouldn't there have been clues? They feel duped and stupid. . .*we should have known.*

Second, empathy: They don't want to believe it because it could happen to any teacher. They know precisely how vulnerable they are. They know exactly how dangerous an angry student or parent can be. Miffed over a low grade or some perceived slight, students and parents have been known to vindictively make accusations based on almost nothing. Sure, there's always an investigation and if the teacher is innocent they'll be proven so. But can a teacher's reputation ever recover? Won't there always be a bit of, "Oh, you know Mr. Smith, the one who was accused of——"?

Third, revulsion: Sexual impropriety of any kind goes against every instinct teachers have, instincts to protect, nurture, and guide. If it's true, and they desperately hope it's not, they want the perpetrator punished to the fullest extent of the law as badly as anyone.

Deep down, they worry that one teacher's crime taints them all. They hate when the profession takes a hit, putting another bullet in the gun of the public-school bashers. Some believe that the problem lies with the teacher unions, that they somehow conspire to protect the unsavory. That's not true, of course. By law, no matter what the profession, union member or not, employees have a right to go through the legal process if accused of a crime.

Most importantly though, how could this person have ended up in a school, our school? Why wasn't there some way to prevent this?

Law enforcement continues to improve the system. Fingerprinting, predator-free zones, background checks, and the Dru Sjodin National Sex Offender Registry coordinated by the Department of Justice have made it more difficult for sex offenders to get into schools.

At this point the concern is not so much how to keep them out.

It's how to recognize the ones who are already inside.

NO SUBSTITUTE FOR A GOOD SUBSTITUTE

Ms. Cleary stepped up to the podium and confidently raised the baton. The students raised their instruments and—a few notes of lovely music segued into an ear-piercing screech and then—abrupt silence. Forty-two bug-eyed students looked at Ms. Cleary in amazement.

Okay, so now she knows. When band directors wave those skinny batons they are not just keeping time to the music. It's actually a highly nuanced set of directions for the musicians to follow.

In her defense let's just say this: She was twenty-three years old, just out of college, and had no music background whatsoever. She was also substitute teaching for the first time. Her delight at being assigned to a music class quickly turned into a good laugh at herself when she realized she had no idea what she was doing.

She fared a bit better in the automotive class the next week. In her skirt and high heels she perched on a grubby garage chair and chatted with a genial group of boys in dirty coveralls while they puttered about with tools.

Such is the plight of the substitute teacher. It's not a job for those who can't think on their feet or go with the flow. The telephone becomes an alarm clock and the calls from sleepy secretaries start at 5 a.m. And a call at the last minute can mean a harrowing drive across town to get to the school on time.

In a perfect world, substitutes are certified teachers assigned to classes in their major. But that almost never happens. Most often subs are not certified teachers at all, but merely warm bodies with enough college credits and a clean background check to allow them to sub in a public school.

Unfortunately, a major in math is usually less important than a major in student discipline. When kids walk past a classroom and see a sub in place of their teacher, news travels fast and the high jinks begin.

Now that substitute teacher positions in many districts have been outsourced to service providers, it's less likely that a district knows well all of its subs. Most schools, though, have a few high quality, dependable subs that are so good teachers clamor to get them. These subs know the clientele, understand the culture, and make every effort to fit in.

But let's face it; sometimes, you really do get what you pay for. Low pay and the transient nature of the job can result in the arrival of some highly interesting characters.

Consider, for example, the young substitute who left his class unattended mid-morning. When word reached the main office that the kids in Room 203 had been left unsupervised, the principal went to the classroom and waited. The sub showed up fifteen minutes later carrying a steaming Burger King bag.

He was shown the door and they never saw him again.

FIRST IMPRESSIONS

All she wanted was to make a really good impression.

After all, she hadn't set foot in her alma mater since graduation on the football field that sweltering day in June.

Just out of college teaching jobs were scarce, so she did what everyone did hoping to get a foot in the door. She registered for the worst job ever: substitute teaching.

And finally, she got The Call: an assignment at her alma mater.

She donned her best new grown-up clothes and took off in her beat-up Mustang. Zipping along, she and Diana Ross sang, getting pumped to face a room full of teenagers.

So lusty was their duet that she didn't hear the siren right away. She didn't notice the red and blue bubble lights flashing behind her, either. And when she did, unfortunately, she was right in front of the school. So naturally, the officer waved her into the parking lot and pulled in behind her.

Shaking with nerves, she stoically endured the lecture about speeding (ten over), silently willing the officer to just hurry up and go away.

Notified of the fact that there was a police car in his school parking lot, of course the principal came out to investigate…and meet the new sub for the first time.

Just when she thought it couldn't get any worse—really—she looked up to see every classroom window filled with pointing, laughing students.

Red-faced and sweaty she hustled in, got her schedule, and settled into first hour. It was a well-organized business class and the kids were on automatic pilot, giving her a minute to settle herself.

Calm at last she strolled up and down the aisles, looking over students' shoulders as they practiced typing business letters. Suddenly, she came upon something that brought the red flooding right back to her face. A young man had a condom on his desk, quite shocking in 1980 when "condom" wasn't yet a household word. Worse, he was carefully unrolling it. Nothing she'd learned in college prepared her for this. Frozen in horror, she tried to think of what to do. Take it away from him? (Yuck!) Or tell him to put it away? She opted for the latter.

Eventually, blissfully, it was lunchtime. She entered the only room she'd never set foot in at her alma mater: the teachers' lounge. She felt every bit of her youth and inexperience as she sat with her former teachers in that forbidden, mysterious place.

"So, you're subbing for Ms. Smith," said one teacher. "That's funny, I don't remember ever seeing her in here at lunch."

The full implication of that didn't register right away.

"What do you mean you never see Ms. Smith in here during this lunch? Are you saying she doesn't have this lunch?" asked another teacher.

"You know," she replied. "I don't think she does."

Holy crap. The secretary had incorrectly written out the schedule and somewhere in the building was a lunch-sprung group of unsupervised teenagers. She dropped her sandwich and bolted.

When she burst through the classroom door she came face to face with her hard-to-impress seventeen-year-old sister, a junior at the school.

Who just rolled her eyes.

Which pretty much summed up the impression she made that day.

ON BEING PUNKED

Teaching can be a humbling experience.

Teenagers womp on a teacher's self-esteem and dignity daily. And no matter how good a teacher is, the things that webcams and cell phone cameras catch can be downright humiliating.

Those black, glassy Orwellian eyes mounted in the ceiling supposedly curb misbehavior and increase security. But tattered teaching egos don't need to have their foibles immortalized for all eternity. Imagine the guy in Security replaying Webcam footage in slow motion for his lunchtime entertainment…

In her mind's eye, Ms. Blume always pictures herself calm and poised, teaching students who are spellbound by her lesson. She is serene. In control. Revered.

The reality often falls far short of that. Whenever Ms. Blume starts to pat herself on the back, something happens to give her self-confidence a good, hard shake.

Her first brush with reality occurred the very first week of her very first year of teaching, long before she grew eyes in the back of her head.

It is Friday, and Ms. Blume sits at her desk, proudly surveying her domain. Her students are taking a test. Except for the slight scratching of pen on paper, the room is silent. All heads are down. Busy. Quiet. Concentrating.

Ah, she thinks. This is good. Very good. She smiles and begins grading papers.

Bonk.

Out of nowhere, a paper airplane sails through the air with the precision of a Patriot missile and scores a direct hit—square on her nose. Her head snaps up. Her eyes pop in disbelief.

A fast look around the room reveals…nothing. Every single student has head bent to paper, diligently working.

Her eyes narrow to slits. She stares and waits. The students keep working.

Carefully she looks at each student, certain that she will see a smirk, a smile, a raised eyebrow.

She watches. She waits.

Nothing. Everyone keeps working.

How the culprit keeps a straight face, she'll never know. And he's still out there, somewhere. A Webcam would have caught him, but it would have caught the airplane bouncing off her nose, too.

Ms. Blume's next brush with reality is even more embarrassing. She is sitting at her desk, a line of students waiting to go over their writing assignments. One by one she talks to them, quickly and competently dispensing advice and information. She is feeling good. Capable. Efficient.

She leans back in her chair to look up at a particularly tall kid.

Crrrr-ack!

Suddenly she is flat on her back, like George Samsa in Kafka's Metamorphosis, legs waving in the air. Her chair has snapped right off of its wheeled base and the entire chair went backward, with her in it. Her arms are even still on the armrests.

She lies there—astounded—looking up at the tall kid who is suddenly even taller. The kid, bless his heart, doesn't even blink.

"Ms. Blume, I can use first person in a personal narrative right? Right?"

So intent is he on getting his question answered that he simply steps to where he can see her better and earnestly talks on.

Perhaps this is just another of the inexplicable actions of the adults in his life. It doesn't even register with him that the she is no longer upright.

The saucer-eyed kids in line behind him snort with laughter. So funny is the sight of their teacher on her back like a bug that it doesn't occur to a single one of them to help her and her pride get up.

On second thought, maybe Webcams aren't such a bad idea. Schools could compile the funny clips and produce a video.

Might start a whole new trend in fund-raising.

THE AGONY AND THE DEFEAT

Students don't know it and parents don't believe it, but assigning a letter grade to a student can be one of the most agonizing, distressing decisions that a teacher makes. No matter how carefully structured the grading system is, or how many safety nets a teacher provides, no one wants to smack a letter label on a kid.

The movie *The Emperor's Club* demonstrates perfectly the reason teachers suffer such acute agony when grades are due, and why the process takes so much longer than it should.

In the movie, Mr. Hundert, a teacher at a prestigious old school for boys, struggles to reach one rebellious student, Sedgewick Bell, the neglected son of an unscrupulous senator. Eventually, he connects with the boy. When Bell finishes one point away from the finals in the Julius Ceasar Contest, an important academic competition, Mr. Hundert gives him the point, hoping to fan the flames of Bell's intellectual curiosity.

Of course it ends badly. Bell cheats during the competition, Mr. Hundert calls him on it, and Bell unashamedly admits it. The fragile bond is broken and Bell returns to his bad boy ways.

It's a variation of a story that's played out repeatedly in schools everywhere as teachers spend hours agonizing over student grades.

Let's say a student's points fall just short of passing, at 59 percent. The teacher ponders the big picture: How many assignments were (or were not) turned in? How was class participation? Tardiness? Attendance? Were there extenuating circumstances, like a death in the family, or illness?

Most importantly, though, what is this student's attitude toward learning? Did they try, or did they slough off until the last minute and then panic? Because that's what matters most to a teacher: that a student be willing to try. Rules will be bent and accommodations will be made for a student who tries.

But it's never an easy decision. Teachers attempt to gaze into a crystal ball to see what the student might learn from this favor. Will he see it as a gift, an opportunity to get his act together and do better? Or will he see it as a way of working the system, a means to an end? Will he think that he's the exception to the rule all his life? Would it be better in the long run to let him feel the consequences of his actions? And in giving one student a break, are we ultimately being unfair to another student?

If it works, and the student learns from the incident, teachers feel buoyant, optimistic, vindicated. But when it doesn't, and a student continues a downhill spiral, teachers feel duped, sad, and profoundly disappointed, in the student and inexplicably, in themselves. It's a personal struggle, one of many that teachers face.

Ultimately Bell just works the system. Several years later, a successful Bell invites Mr. Hundert to facilitate a rematch of the Julius Caesar Contest, and he cheats again.

As Mr. Hundert says, "However much we stumble, it is a teacher's burden always to hope, that with learning, a boy's character might be changed, and so the destiny of a man."

Teachers, regardless of the burden, never cease to hope.

A SNOW DAY IS A HOLIDAY

It is sixth hour. Snow is falling heavily and Bob's eyes keep straying to the clock. If this keeps up, he thinks, there's no way we'll have school tomorrow.

Suddenly, there's an interruption on the PA. Everyone freezes, listening intently.

"MAY I HAVE YOUR ATTENTION PLEASE. THE WEATHER SERVICE HAS ISSUED A WINTER STORM WARNING IN EFFECT UNTIL EIGHT O'CLOCK TOMORROW MORNING. PLEASE LISTEN TO YOUR LOCAL TELEVISION STATIONS AND CHECK OUR WEBSITE IN THE EVENT THAT SCHOOL MAY BE CANCELED TOMORROW."

Yes!

Bob begins gathering up his things. The bell rings and everyone rushes into the hall, chattering excitedly.

When Bob gets home he turns on the TV. Hmm. . . nothing yet. He goes to the school's website. Nothing there either. Well, there's still time. He sets his cell phone on the table next to him, just in case.

He goes to the window and looks out. About three inches of snow cover the ground, and it is still coming down heavily, in big, fat, fluffy flakes. He sits and watches for a while.

He wonders about the test that is scheduled for tomorrow. He thinks about doing his schoolwork, and wonders if he dares skip it. If he doesn't have school tomorrow, he can get caught up then. Or not. Maybe he'll lie on the couch and watch TV all day. No doubt he'll have to shovel, but it's worth it if he doesn't have school.

He goes back to the TV and sits down on the couch. He watches the crawl across the bottom of the screen. Some evening activities and sporting events are canceled. No schools yet, though. He can't seem to pull his eyes away from that crawl.

After dinner, Bob goes online and checks the school's website again, and then the local TV station's website. The list is growing, but his school still isn't there.

What if we're the only school that's not called off, he thinks. *It's happened before. Oh, that would be so disappointing.*

He goes back to the TV. Hmm. . . maybe if he switches to another station. Still nothing.

He watches the crawl for a while longer. He wonders which roads the superintendent drives when he goes out to check them. He wonders what code word the superintendent uses when he calls the media to cancel school.

Feeling restless, he pulls on his boots and goes outside. He looks up and down the street. It is coming down so hard that the streetlight a block away is barely visible. No sign of a salt truck. No sign of a plow. Good. He takes a few experimental steps in the snow. Then he runs and takes an all-out slide across the driveway, skidding to a stop. *All right*, he thinks. *It's slippery under all that snow.*

When he comes in, Bob calls his buddy Steve.

"Have you heard anything yet?" he asks.

"No, not yet," Steve says.

"Well, call me the minute you hear," Bob says.

"OK, you do the same," Steve replies.

It grows late, and Bob knows he should go to bed or he'll be tired tomorrow. I'll just watch TV a few more minutes, he thinks. He puts the remote and his cell phone next to his bed in case he wants to check in the night.

He closes his eyes and tries to sleep. Six hours later he awakes with a start, well before his alarm goes off, and reaches immediately for the remote. He holds his breath and counts to ten superstitiously. OK, he thinks, it's got to be there now. He turns on the TV and starts reading the crawl, still holding his breath.

Aha! There it is! Yes! The first official snow day of the year!

Bob turns off the TV and burrows back down under the covers.

And silently thanks God that he teaches at a school that doesn't require teachers to report on snow days.

AH, IN-SERVICE: THANKS FOR THE NAP

Martin Luther King Day makes some teachers shudder.

In communities, Martin Luther King Day is an opportunity to honor a great American. And for students, it's a day off school and a trip to the mall. But for teachers, Martin Luther King Day means only one thing: the dreaded in-service.

The first problem with in-services is that reluctant teachers, already juggling too many tasks, are strong-armed by administrators into "volunteering" to plan them. So at the end of a long day of teaching they meet and, armed with good intentions, little time, and almost no budget, struggle to plan an enlightening and inspiring day for their colleagues.

It's a thankless job.

The second problem with in-services, regardless of who plans them, is that once the educational community comes up with a new educational theory, they beat it to death. The simplest concept is dragged out interminably. For example, teachers might learn about multiple learning styles at an in-service. It's wonderfully useful, but it's not rocket science. They understand it the first time it's presented. They don't need to be drilled on it repeatedly for the next three years.

Yet they are.

The third problem with in-services is that teachers are treated like children instead of professionals. They're often put into groups when they arrive to ensure that they don't sit with their friends. Building principals strategically place themselves around the room so teachers can't grade papers while they listen. And if they happen to get through the in-service material early, administrators scramble to fill the time with inane announcements, rather than let them go early.

The most demoralizing thing about in-services, though, is that so much of the time is spent pointing out where teachers are supposedly not succeeding. Sometimes, each teacher's students' collective grade point averages are passed out (they're too low). Sometimes it's standardized test scores (too low, too). Sometimes it's discipline referrals (much too high).

"Bam!" goes another nail, right into the teaching spirit's coffin.

The one thing that teachers need more than anything is quiet time to work in their classrooms (on the clock for a change, not after school). They also want time with their colleagues to share lessons and discipline strategies. Truly, sometimes the most teachers see of their colleagues is a wave as they pass in the hall, or a quick hello at the bathroom sink. Yet that seems to be the one thing that administrators and school boards are most loath to give. Instead, teachers are treated as if they can't be trusted with any unstructured time and in-services are packed full of busywork. There's a strong Puritan work ethic in education that fears a few idle minutes.

It's not that there isn't anything new to be learned. There is. And teachers don't object to learning it. But just like their students, they do object to busywork.

So why do teachers put up with it? Why don't they just put their collective aching feet down? Mostly, it's because teachers are basically follow-the-rules kinds of people.

There's a much more compelling reason, though, an epiphany that comes after a particularly bad week of inadvertently giving too many writing assignments at once resulting in stacks of essays to grade, on top of several nerve-wracking conferences with parents, and three after-school meetings in a row. They are worn out and then…

It hits them. Tomorrow is…In-Service Day! Someone else will have to create the lesson, type the handouts, stand on their feet and deliver the material! Teachers can sit and…rest!

That's why teachers suffer in-services in silence. They're just so blasted grateful to have someone else run the show for a while.

But one thing is certain. After an all-day in-service, they're pretty thrilled to get back to their classrooms.

It can make that really rowdy third hour class look pretty darn good.

FASTEN YOUR SEAT BELTS

"This isn't Disney World, people! These aren't bumper cars! I want to see six—car—lengths—between you!"

Welcome to The Range, where driver's education students perfect daring skills like lane changes and backing up. Meet Mr. Brave and Mr. Calm, two intrepid driver's training instructors who soothe students' giddy nerves with the antics of a good cop/bad cop comedy team.

Mr. Brave begins the lesson by walking students over the course on foot. They follow like puppies, nearly piling up Three Stooges style when he stops. He could tell them to yodel and they would, so eager are they to please this man who holds the keys to freedom. Every one becomes a model student, including the ones who spent most of the year in detention.

With warm-hearted exasperation Mr. Brave hollers through his bullhorn a mix of encouragement and skepticism as students attempt a serpentine around cones—going backward.

"No! No! No!" he yells, shaking his head, hand smacking his forehead. "Jeezopeets, what the heck was *that*?" he mutters as a car backs squarely over a cone, tearing it in half.

It's hot on the range, over an acre of asphalt throbbing in the heat of a relentless July sun. The sweating instructors are on high alert every minute, preaching safety, trotting miles alongside cars, giving instructions through the open window to the white-knuckled students behind the wheel as they pilot that Chevrolet at five terrifying miles an hour.

And then, it's time to leave the range. Everyone buckles up as Mr. Calm prepares to take two students for their road debut. Everything that seems so charmingly comical on the range—herky jerky stops, jack-rabbit starts and close turns around orange cones that drop like bowling pins—is terribly unnerving on a real road with fast traffic.

With the serene, reassuring tone of a chatty airline pilot, Mr. Calm keeps up a steady stream of instruction and encouragement, even during the rather hair-raising passing of a tractor. Fortunately, the students tucked into the back seat can't see much over a headrest the size of a mattress. They have a perfect view of the steering wheel, however, and a clear shot every time Mr. Calm's hand shoots out to grab it and guide them back onto the pavement.

While ninety minutes flies by for the students, the time passes more slowly for Mr. Calm. But by the end of the lesson both drivers are visibly more comfortable behind the wheel.

Adults take their driving skills for granted, things like the ability to talk and maintain speed at the same time, or stop at a stop sign and not ten yards short of it. Or simply keeping it between the lines.

Those driver education teachers are a marvel. They think not a thing about getting into a fast car on a busy road with an adolescent kid who has yet to clip his first mailbox.

It's not a job for sissies.

BURNOUT, SECRECY, AND DENIAL

They're not going to admit it to you. They probably haven't even admitted it to themselves. But there are hundreds of classroom teachers, right this minute, living lives of quiet desperation.

It's called teacher burnout and it's an affliction of secrecy and denial. In a profession that by its very nature requires a person to be upbeat and positive all the time, and in fact offers no place to hide when they aren't, to not be so is to fail.

And let's face it; society isn't always kind when people admit their weaknesses. Several years ago on *The Oprah Winfrey Show*, new mothers discussed their inability to get into the groove of motherhood. They hadn't felt the bliss that other mothers did. The blissful mothers' unforgiving attitude was, what kind of freak is unhappy with a brand new baby?

Society can be unkind to those who don't feel the way they "should."

Which is why, even when overwhelmed by it, teachers often deny their despair. They don't want to look weak or reflect badly on their school. It's depressing and frightening when your calling, no longer is.

Some call teaching the lonely profession because teachers spend their days closed away in classrooms with kids and have little or no contact with adults.

And that's true. If you ask a retired teacher if they miss their colleagues, they're likely to say no. Not because they don't like them. They do. But they don't miss what they never had. There's little time in a teacher's day for chitchat. A quick hello in the lunch line doesn't a friendship make. Even the half-hour lunch leaves little time for collegiality. And many teachers eat in their classrooms so they can give kids extra help.

In fact, when asked what kind of professional development they want, teachers say they want time to spend with their colleagues, to share teaching and discipline strategies, or to get answers to simple questions like, "How do you make prepositions interesting?" or "What do you do when the same kid forgets his textbook for the tenth time in a row?"

Feeling like they have no say in decisions that affect them, struggling to make kids care about education, little evidence that they've made a difference to their students, and plain and simple exhaustion all lead to burnout.

But once they've spent a great deal of time and money earning several degrees, and have moved up the pay scale, changing careers is daunting.

Too many burned-out teachers stay on the job, detached and not connecting with kids. There should be some sort of assistance program for career teachers who don't want to leave, but need help getting their fire relit.

Because if there's no help and they can't leave, unfortunately, they're taking up space where an inspired teacher could be.

TIME TO FLY

Search your soul, teacher: Is it time for you to retire?

You think it's no one's business but your own. And it's a painful, touchy subject.

When you look around at the new crop of teachers, you're thinking that even on your worst day you're better than most of them. And that may be a little bit true. At least you've got your classroom under control, which is more than can be said for many rookies, right?

But think back. You didn't always have your classroom under control that first year, either. That came with experience. You learned that kids are like animals that sense fear. When you quit showing that fear, they quit testing you.

Bet you know your subject better than those newbies, too, don't you? You've had years to steep yourself in your material, and they're barely a chapter ahead of the kids. In time, those things will come to the rookies. But you know as well as anybody that there's more to good teaching than classroom control and mastery of subject.

Are you still creative, or are you in a rut? Are you using ancient lesson plans and tests? Have you chalked up all new teaching methods as just so much "edubabble"? Are there any new challenges for you in the classroom? Are you still able and willing to challenge the kids?

Are you letting a responsible student do too much of your work, like taking attendance and entering grades? Do you give fewer assignments because you don't want to grade them? Are you spending more time in the teachers' lounge lounging than working?

Are you bored? If so, chances are you're boring, too.

Are you more easily frustrated than you used to be? More impatient? Less tolerant? Have you lost that most sustaining of qualities—your sense of humor?

Are you starting to believe there's no hope for this generation? Have you stopped believing that you make a difference? Have you quit trying to reach each and every kid?

Are you just there for the paycheck?

Most importantly, how is your heart? Is it still wide open to each and every student? Don't answer that too quickly. There's a difference between wholehearted passion and just marking time.

And this is about passion, not age. You can teach 'til you're ninety if your passion is still obvious to the kids. Because just as they sensed your fear as a rookie, they sense your apathy now. And that's why you must leave; apathy breeds apathy.

It's scary. You've lived by the school calendar your whole entire life and you're wondering what you will be if you're no longer a teacher. But know this: You'll always be a teacher at heart.

If you see yourself here, turn in your retirement papers.

Sometimes there's more valor in leaving than in staying.

THE BURNING BUSH

Flames shot from the branches. Dark smoke billowed.

She stared at that burning bush for a moment, as sure as Moses that it was some kind of sign.

Of what, she was not sure.

Then she sprang into action, raced to the phone, and called the main office. "Students set fire to the bushes on the north side of the building," she said. "Get someone out there, quick."

By the time she got back to the window a principal and a custodian were on the scene. The buses had left and all was quiet. Certain that things were under control, she dropped into her desk chair.

What just happened here? she thought, and she didn't just mean the burning bush. She meant, what happened in this room for the last ten months?

For it was the last day of her first year of teaching, and while the kids celebrated by playing pyromaniac, she celebrated by sitting down at her desk for what felt like the first time all year.

Introspection and reflection are luxuries teachers have no time for. From the moment they hit the door in the morning, until they drag out to their cars at night, they hustle to respond to student needs: "I need a Kleenex, do you have a Band-aid, my paper ripped, he hit me, he took my book, I forgot my book, I lost my book, what page are we on, I don't have a pencil, I hate this class, it's too hot in here, it's too cold in here, I'm tired, I'm bored, I'm mad!"

That first year she felt consumed by details. She felt like a parrot, destined to repeat "Don't forget to put your name on your paper" for the rest of her life. Much of the year she operated on autopilot, trying to stay one step, one assignment, one tear, one tantrum, one giggling fit ahead of her ninth graders.

She felt like she could sleep for a week.

She had just said a bittersweet goodbye to those ninth graders. She was so sad to see most of them go, though not, in all honesty, all of them. She worried about the trouble they might find over the hormone-hot summer.

As she gazed at the tattered bulletin boards and littered floor, she saw in her mind's eye all of the drama that had played itself out in this room.

And in the way of teachers everywhere, her mind wandered to next year, to new ways to present old material, to streamline systems, to better connect with her students. She began jotting notes in her planbook.

She glanced out the window. The bush was not consumed.

And neither was she.

IT'S NOT A JOB, IT'S A CALLING

Dear Jamie,

You wrote asking my advice about a career in education. I'll answer you as honestly as I can.

I loved teaching. I did not leave education because I was down on kids. The kids were fine. I felt privileged to know them, and honored to play even a small role in their development. In fact, I'm still in touch with many of them and consider them friends. No, I left education because the job was consuming me. I was burned-out and there are no resources for burned out teachers.

What caused the burnout? Well, what eventually wore me down was the number of people I had to answer to: the kids, their parents, administrators, politicians. I always felt that with fewer students I could have been extraordinary. But the masses overwhelmed me.

I'm a Type A perfectionist, but there is no perfect in education. It's a murky, blurry business and you rarely know for sure that you've done it right. Each child is unique and has wildly different needs. There's not enough time in the day, though, to figure out who needs what, and to meet all of those needs, which left me feeling inadequate a lot of the time.

You should not choose to teach because you "get summers off." That may have been true in the past, but it's not any longer. If you teach, the rest of your summers will be filled with workshops and classes to maintain your certification.

It's important that you really know yourself and what working conditions you need to thrive. As a teacher you will rarely be alone or have quiet, contemplative time. You must be physically strong and healthy because the pace is relentless, on your feet and projecting your voice all day. You must be a master of organization and have a high tolerance for repetition. But if you teach, your co-workers will be some of the most highly principled people you'll ever meet in your life.

Most of what you need to be a good teacher can be learned, much from experience. But some inherent personality traits will allow you to flourish in the classroom, such as a sincere love of people, patience, optimism, and a good sense of humor. You cannot be thin-skinned or in constant need of approval. If there's a bit of the performer in you, if you relish being a role model, if you can easily handle not only volumes of paperwork but also volumes of people, then life in the classroom is for you.

And that light-bulb moment that teachers talk about? That moment when a kid really gets it? That is truly pure and splendid and can make all the rest worthwhile.

Teaching is not just a job. It's a calling. You can't do it any way but wholeheartedly.

So, Jamie, if you're thinking about teaching, perhaps the universe is trying to tell you something. Teach only because you were born to. It's a noble and honorable profession.

As for me, would I do it all again?

Absolutely.

With love,

Your former teacher

Chapter Two

Students

From facing resistance and trashed bathrooms to cologne in the eye and getting skunked

Tell me and I forget. Teach me and I remember. Involve me and I learn.

—Benjamin Franklin

COLOGNE BOY

He pressed his knuckles into his eyes and scrubbed furiously.

"How about now?" he asked. "Are they red now?"

"Stop it, leave your eyes alone," his teacher said. "I mean it. Stop it."

"Yeah, but if I can get them red enough, they'll send me home. I heard that if you get pinkeye, they send you home. I want to go home."

The boy ground his knuckles into his eyes even harder.

"That's not good for your eyes. Just stop it," repeated the teacher.

The boy kept rubbing.

"How about now? How red are they now?"

"*Stop it*! I mean it, stop that *right now*!" the teacher said firmly.

Suddenly, the boy's hand darted into his backpack and he pulled out a bottle of cologne (the standard alternative to a shower after gym class).

And quick as lightning he flipped the top off the bottle and sprayed himself, right in the eye.

And then he howled.

And then he got to go home.

True story. And the reason it's important is because it's such a bizarre story, and one that speaks to the absurdity of life in a public school, where teachers strive to educate every stratum of society.

Some educators would not share a story like that. It goes against their instinct to protect the reputation of public schools. Many educators only want to share stories about the hours of inspiring lessons that go well and smoothly, where teaching and learning thrive. They feel that when the media latches on to an odd incident or violent episode in a public school, it taints the entire system.

It's important to look at the big picture, though, including the bizarre, because that's where you find the inexplicable minutiae that compromise the learning environment. And test scores.

Too many people imagine that students behave like they did in the 1950s, sitting tall and straight in their chairs, offering teachers their undivided attention.

And if that's how it's imagined then ideas about how to "fix" education will completely miss the mark. For the education reform conversation to be effective, it's important to see the issues clearly.

People need to know exactly why the twenty-first century classroom is so darned challenging.

They need to see all of it. From the ridiculous, to the sublime.

DISCIPLINE? OH, IT'S NEVER EASY

No matter how experienced teachers may be, they never discipline a student without secretly second-guessing themselves and wondering whether or not they handled it right.

The self-doubt can be tormenting. Take, for example, that nonstop talker. The teacher moves her to three different seats, then worries: Did changing her seat embarrass the child? Or did she love the attention? Could she have been teased into cooperating? Should her mom have been called the very first time she disrupted class? Was it unfair to the quiet kid to move that talker next to him?

And what about that nice boy who had his pocketknife out on his desk? He didn't think of it as a weapon. To him, it was just a little pocketknife, like the ones his dad and grandpa carried. But zero tolerance is zero tolerance, and he got expelled. Did the teacher dare look the other way?

Even strict teachers with well-managed classrooms, the ones who handle all of their own discipline and never send students to the principal's office, experience doubt.

And it's always stressful. Worrying about students' delicate psyches is what keeps teachers lying awake until long past midnight. It's what they think about in the car on the way to school, and on the way home again at night. It's what they talk about—endlessly, unceasingly, perpetually, ad infinitum—to their spouses, and friends, and colleagues in the lounge, looking for advice, comfort, or validation. And though they may appear calm and firm in front of their students, behind closed doors they gnash their teeth and worry.

Should they have been tougher on Jason? Easier on Amanda? Have they somehow scarred this child for life? Will this discipline foster a healthy respect? Or will it shut down the child so completely that he won't learn anything else all year? Is there a lesson in this discipline? Has she learned it? Or is the teacher just spinning her wheels?

Student behavior is a monstrous issue for school districts. The general public can't imagine the time and energy that is spent—wasted—on student discipline every single day. If a wave of the magic wand could make discipline issues disappear, every school would make adequate yearly progress and teachers would never burn out.

So if your phone rings this marking period, and a school official is on the other end of the line, please know this: That person wants what's best for your child. But they're also responsible for maintaining a positive learning environment for every child.

Trust that they're doing their best to be fair and consistent.

And know that it's never, ever easy.

TAKE BACK THE HALLS

Four words describe how to improve every school in this country: Take back the halls.

In some schools, on some days, the general public would be shocked at how students behave in the halls between classes. While many move peacefully and mind their own business, far too many think hall time is party time, and that hall behavior has nothing to do with classroom behavior. Simple requests to stop running, remove hats, put away cell phones, or stop swearing are greeted with a "make me" attitude, which is second only to the "you can't make me" attitude.

Ideally, every adult in the building supervises the halls during passing time. In reality, that almost never happens. For teachers, those five precious minutes are often spent on a quick run to the restroom, a sprint to the office to make a copy, readying the room for the next class, catching up a student who's been absent, returning a parent's phone call, taking AV equipment back to the media center, consulting with another teacher. The list is varied and endless.

But a strong unified front during the first week of school would go a long way toward setting appropriate expectations. Picture this: On the very first day of school every teacher, hall monitor and principal is posted throughout the halls, with the most adults concentrated near the main student entrances. The minute the doors open, students are greeted warmly, and then every single infraction is corrected, swiftly and firmly. Food and beverages are thrown away, hats are removed, dress code violations are busted, cell phones are confiscated—whatever it takes. Send a strong, clear message in the *very first minutes* of the new school year that there are expectations, and they will be enforced.

Period.

Then tell students that the infractions will be removed from their records in twelve weeks if they have no other in-school violations.

The problem is, teachers and administrators alike sometimes look the other way if they're too busy or too tired to enforce a rule. Unfortunately, it's not unusual to see a student carry a soft drink or wear a hat right past a principal or a teacher.

And make no mistake, that urge to look the other way can be strong. When Ms. Button, a gregarious, fun-loving teacher known for her ability to make eerily realistic sound effects when teaching onomatopoeia to her freshman English students, opened her classroom door to get some fresh air, she came face to face with a sight that left her momentarily speechless. A girl and a boy were standing in the hall with their tongues stretched out of their mouths, rubbing them together.

Shocked, and more than a little grossed out, her first impulse was to turn on her heel and pretend she didn't see it. Instead, she issued a reprimand and then endured the rolled eyes, heavy sighs, and snide mutterings of the put-upon students.

If school rules are enforced haphazardly—and they are—it sends the message that those rules are not important. But if the goal is teaching and learning, the learning environment must be sacred. Teachers, administrators, and parents must insist on it.

If kids run wild in the halls, it's the adults who are to blame. A well-disciplined school is a choice. A choice not made by students, but by the adults in charge of those students.

The entire country is focused on higher standards in education. But that focus is largely trained on test scores. If we want students to take education seriously, educators must start by insisting that the learning environment be inviolate. Parents need to step up to the plate and support that, too.

And the place to start is in the halls.

JUST USE YOUR SLEEVE

Why is it that every high school kid's book bag holds an iPod, a cell phone, and a twenty-ounce Coke, but no Kleenex?

Things get ugly fast during cold and flu season in public schools, because there's never enough Kleenex to go around. That means teachers spend their own money to supply them. They have to. It's either that, or fight the gag reflex all day listening to kids snork it up.

Seems like a small thing, doesn't it?

"Gee whiz, what's the big deal, it's only a Kleenex! Give the kid a Kleenex if he needs it!"

But it gets expensive. The average class goes through at least a box a week. Even if they're the scratchy cheapies bought on sale, it's over a buck a box. Multiply that by approximately thirty-eight weeks, and a teacher is spending a minimum of $50 a year on classroom Kleenex. Multiply that by twenty years and, there goes the round-trip ticket to Jamaica.

Most districts purchase some tissues, but they usually run out before the first marking period is over. If the district supplied enough Kleenex for everyone all year long, there wouldn't be money for textbooks.

Some teachers get creative, though. One teacher swipes a roll of toilet paper from the bathroom and puts it on his desk. Another provides a stack of rough brown industrial paper towels from the dispenser in the teachers' lounge. Some choose to ignore the wishes of their building principals and take the time to write passes to the bathroom all day, creating a steady stream of unsupervised hall traffic.

Some don't do anything. No Kleenex, no passes, nothing but your sleeve, kid.

Some students wouldn't use Kleenex even if they had them. Take Elliott for example. (Not his real name, for reasons that will become obvious.) This freshman sits in the back of the classroom every day with his fingers up his nose to the knuckles. When he finally gets what he's after, he eats it.

Seriously.

So there's a building full of kids and a severe Kleenex shortage.

Now take all of the soap out of the bathrooms. High school bathrooms never have soap or paper towels, because some students consider it to be high sport to dump them on the floor.

So the kids can't wash their hands and the germs have a free-for-all on every doorknob in the place. They're positively greasy. Every desk, every locker, every textbook, every surface in a school building is just creepy-crawly with ick.

If a teacher puts the Kleenex on her desk so she can monitor the supply, she faces a steady stream of kids coughing, sneezing, sniffing and honking in her face. All day. If she moves the Kleenex away from her desk, they wait 'til she's not looking and stuff their pockets with enough tissues to get them through the day, further depleting the meager provisions.

But the little old gray-haired career teacher down the hall has a tissue trick that she shares with all the new teachers. When a student asks her for a Kleenex she rummages around in her purse for a minute, then finally pulls out a wrinkled, wadded-up tissue. She gives it a little shake, hands it to the kid and says, "Here. I'm pretty sure it's clean."

They never ask again.

FAILING ABDUL

For teachers, it is one of the most frustrating things they'll ever experience. They feel inadequate. Deficient. Neglectful. Helpless.

If the teacher feels that way, imagine how the student feels.

Abdul came into his freshman English class speaking not one word of English. None, nada, zip, zilch (all words he didn't know).

There was no translator. No cue cards. No cheat sheets. This young man had been sent to a school where he could not communicate at all with the people around him. He couldn't ask for a Kleenex. He couldn't tell someone if he had a stomachache. He couldn't even ask to go to the bathroom.

For an entire year Abdul and Ms. MacDougall lived in a world of pantomime, exaggerated gestures, and dramatic facial expressions, using eyebrows to communicate—raised in question, scowling in misunderstanding, knit in consternation. Because of cultural differences she dared not even pat his back in reassurance.

The county educational service agency provided a tutor for Abdul. He was scheduled to work with Abdul for one whole hour a week. And in that meager amount of time, try to help Abdul with all six of his classes.

Ms. MacDougall couldn't even call Abdul's parents for a conference because they didn't speak English either. It is doubtful that his parents expected him to learn the content his classes offered, though. Most likely they hoped that he would learn English simply by being exposed to it for seven hours a day.

On September 11, 2001, the principal came on the PA and instructed teachers to turn their classroom monitors to CNN. As they watched the horror unfold, one by one the students' eyes slid over to Abdul, back to the screen, then back to Abdul. There's no way to know how much of what he saw on TV Abdul understood. But he didn't need English to read the cool speculation in the other students' eyes.

Ms. MacDougall was confounded by how to grade him. She taught English. The students were graded on how much they learned in English. Abdul spoke no English. If she'd had seven hours to spend with Abdul every day, she could have taught him to read. But she didn't. She had twenty-six other students in that hour alone—twenty-six lively freshmen with a multitude of personalities and needs. She was busy every minute trying to keep them engaged and on task.

At the end of first marking period she could tell that Abdul was disappointed with his report card. His tutor, a kind man with warm brown eyes whose workload was as heavy as hers, told her that Abdul had earned the highest grades at his former school. She suspected as much; she could see the light of intelligence in his eyes.

Ms. MacDougall often wonders what happened to Abdul. Did he go back to his home country? Did he have any pleasant memories at all of his time in the American public school?

One thing is certain, though. She could have given Abdul a perfect example of irony, something they covered in that freshman English class.

He was eager to learn, but couldn't. Many of his American classmates could learn, but wouldn't.

COWLICKS, COMBS, AND LIPSTICK

"Cheese!"

It's Picture Day, that visual documentation of a child's growth and development, those endearingly goofy photos chronicling the full gamut of growing pains: braces, bad skin, oversized noses, satellite dish ears, and every sort of fashion faux pas.

And as is so often true, what happens behind the camera is much more telling, and more interesting, than what happens in front of it.

It's a day of high excitement as kids arrive dressed in their finest and fanciest, more appropriate for church or a dance than a day at school.

They don't really get it, but this head-to-toe regalia is overkill, because little more than their neck and shoulders will show in the photo.

They're earnest and intense though, and giddy with anticipation. Hours of plotting and planning have gone into this three-second photo-op, and on this day, even the boys are groomed.

But the girls—oh, the girls! Hoping to look hot, but too often not, freshmen totter around on unfamiliar heels, awkwardly tugging on too-short skirts, patting carefully constructed hair. It's one long day of primping, fussing, smoothing, brushing, combing, posing, and self-conscious preening.

Mirrors, mirrors everywhere. Those without plead for a bathroom pass, adding to the administrative headache of hall traffic and noise.

If it rains on picture day the chaos swells as hair-dos wilt, clothes wrinkle, and faces turn shiny.

Students are offered advice before picture day, though few, unfortunately, take it: Wear a color you look good in. A crewneck T-shirt in a flattering color is better than a dressy outfit in an unflattering color. If you're acne-prone avoid pink and red, as blemishes will only look redder. And skip the complicated, unnatural and unflattering up-dos; your everyday style is most likely more becoming.

Lesson plans are shattered by those endless PA announcements, as kids are herded alphabetically to the photo area, so teachers do their best to plan activities that can tolerate relentless disruptions. If they don't roll with it, those incessant PA announcements will have them begging for mercy.

This unbridled enthusiasm will be revived again when the photo packets arrive. Then it's nearly another lost day as kids happily share and compare, giggle and gush, begging for scissors so they can divvy up the goods. Some go so fast parents never see what they paid for.

The results are as good as can be expected in a cattle call process where time is of the essence. But in the split second that the camera flashes so much can go wrong. A smile becomes a sneer, a grin becomes a leer, a blink becomes closed eyes, or an expression turned wry.

Which is why parents everywhere say, *thank goodness for retakes.*

LOST IN THE CROWD

She sits somewhere in the middle of the classroom.

She's quiet. She's polite. She doesn't contribute to class discussions. She doesn't have many friends and she doesn't get in trouble. She does her schoolwork most of the time, on time. It's not awful, or outstanding.

She doesn't participate in extracurricular activities. She comes to school and rides the bus home, never staying for a meeting or a practice.

Her looks are average. Not homely. Not beautiful. Nothing much distinguishes her from anyone else.

This is the average child. The middle child. And because she neither excels nor fails she gets less attention than the spectacular, or the spectacularly bad, child.

Reams of legislation are passed, and billions of dollars are spent, to protect and nurture the academically challenged children. And precocious, talented, high achieving children naturally command their share of the spotlight. But in the classroom, as in many families, the middle children never seem to get their due.

A well-intentioned teacher makes a deal with a truant student to improve his attendance. "If you come to school for two weeks straight I'll buy you a pizza for lunch," he says.

The average child overhears. "I come to school every day," she says. "What do I get?"

Often, the middle children prefer their anonymity, especially the painfully shy. Their eyes plead with their teachers to let them hide quietly behind their books. It seems most kind to let them.

A wise, experienced teacher cautions new teachers to make sure to spend a few moments with those quiet children each day, to make a point of offering a comment or praise. If you don't, she says, they might fall through the cracks.

Tragically, like busy parents trying to juggle too much, teachers don't always get around to having that quiet moment with the middle children. In one fifty-five-minute period they're pulled in twenty-eight different directions. And then there's that five-pound textbook to get through, and reams of documentation to complete. Backtalkers, spitball throwers, cell phone sneakers, homework deadbeats, bad attitudes, class clowns—and yes, the high-achieving perfectionists—all take time and attention away from the average child.

At the end of the year, the teacher feels bad about every middle child that did not get enough of her attention. If there is one single thing she wishes she had done differently, it would be to close the textbook, set aside the lesson plan, stop rushing, and sit right down with that quiet child.

"What are you thinking about?" she would ask.

And she would listen hard for the answer.

IT'S THE RESISTANCE THAT GETS TO YOU

Resistance.

That's what makes teaching so gosh-darned hard. A sometimes subtle, sometimes in-your-face resistance that's insidious and unrelenting. It makes even the simplest tasks gargantuan. And by the end of that first semester, teachers feel like they've spent ninety days pushing a tank out of the mud.

It works like this. On the way to first hour the teacher spots a student in the hall wearing a cap, a blatant violation of the dress code. She walks up to the student and politely asks him to remove it. Sometimes she's met with a mean glare. Sometimes it escalates into an all-out confrontation, simply because she made an effort to enforce a school rule that has been in place forever. And sometimes the offender waits until she turns away and puts the cap right back on, causing an instant spike to her blood pressure.

The halls are full of such rule breakers, but teachers learn to pick and choose their battles. Who needs unsolicited resistance?

And then there are a dozen daily head-banging conversations like this:

Johnny: "It's not my fault I was late. My ride was late picking me up."

Teacher: "Unless you have a pass in your hand, it's counted as a tardy."

Johnny: "But it's not my fault. My ride was late."

Teacher: "Tardy means you were not here when the last bell rang. That's what tardy is."

Johnny: "But it's *not my fault*! My *ride* was *late*!"

There are infinite variations of that theme: "I shouldn't have to pay for that textbook, it was stolen from me." "I had to run full speed through the hall, otherwise I'd be late." "I forgot my backpack so I can't do any work." "It's not my fault I couldn't do my homework, I wasn't home last night."

And on and on and on.

There's also the resistance teachers meet when they ask students to do something routine. Say "Take out your books and turn to page forty" and they're greeted with every sort of sigh, groan, eye-roll, and under-the-breath grumbling: "Man, this is so boring, why do we always have to do work, why can't we have a free day, why can't school be fun, all we ever do is work, I'm too tired, I'm so bored, I hate this class, man, this *sucks*!"

They resist responsibility, too. Their grade is never their fault. No matter how little work they've done, or what the grade book shows in black and white, a low grade is always because the teacher doesn't like them.

It's like swimming up a waterfall. By the end of the day you're drained, tapped out, bone-tired from fighting against all of that resistance.

But if resistance is the disease, tenacity is the cure. Resistance doesn't stand a chance, because there's no more tenacious person on earth than a teacher.

And besides, at the end of the day all it takes is one friendly student to pop their head in and say cheerfully, "See you tomorrow, Ms. Flynn!"

And she smiles in anticipation.

FULL MOONS AND FRIDAYS

"MAY I HAVE YOUR ATTENTION, PLEASE. IF YOU ATE THE TO-MATO SOUP AT LUNCH TODAY, PLEASE COME TO THE MAIN OF-FICE IMMEDIATELY. I REPEAT, IF YOU ATE THE TOMATO SOUP AT LUNCH TODAY, PLEASE COME TO THE MAIN OFFICE IMMEDI-ATELY."

The announcement comes over the PA halfway through sixth hour. After a moment of stunned silence, every class in the building explodes into laughter, the crescendo echoing down the halls. It's a moment right out of *Porky's*, to be sure.

It's not so funny for the poor souls trudging in trepidation to the office. Turns out the principal got a tip that someone slipped Ex-Lax into the soup at lunch. Luckily, no one gets sick and everyone has a good laugh at the absurdity of life in a school.

Of course it was a Friday. Everything odd happens on Friday. Fist fights, drug busts, bomb threats, false fire alarms, ranting parents, so many kids in trouble that it's standing room only in the main office—always on a Friday.

Every school has a rhythm, a flow, a certain feeling in the air when all is well. And the people who work there intuitively know when it's about to be disrupted. When disruption looms, the air crackles with expectation, putting teachers on high alert. They pass each other in the halls, eyebrows raised, whispering, "What's up? What's going on? Is there a full moon?" They watch their students more closely, peek into the hall more often, just a little more observant, a little more aware.

Because full moons and Fridays are when legends are born.

The time a freshman girl in first hour burst into tears, creating a weird chain reaction that caused every other girl to burst into tears, too—happened on a Friday. The time a thick braid of hair with the barrette still intact was found on the classroom floor after two freshmen girls were hauled off to the office for a truly feral fistfight—happened on a Friday. The time a student climbed out of the classroom window and into a car waiting at the curb—to the delight of passers-by—happened on a Friday.

Teachers are not immune, either. Ms. Shapiro looked out the classroom window during her planning hour and saw a parent she had been trying to reach for weeks parked at the curb. She really wanted to talk to this parent, but knew the car would be long gone by the time she got all the way down the hall and out the door.

Imagine that parent's surprise when she looked up to see the teacher from Room 102 come feet first out of the window and sprint across the lawn.

Yeah, of course. It was Friday.

NOT A HERO

From the teaching journal . . .

She feels like a rotten teacher.

She keeps thinking that if she just tries a little bit harder, if she's kinder, more understanding, more compassionate, more creative, more strict, more *something*, she can fix things in her second hour.

Through luck of the draw the kids in this class are all friends and neighbors who grew up together in the same trailer park. She gathers from their conversations that they party together almost every night. They're only freshmen, but this partying includes booze.

Lots of it.

Absenteeism is high. They aren't here to learn. They are here because it's something they have to get through until tonight's party.

This group is more tightly knit than George W.'s brow, and they follow one leader. His name is Roberto and he wears enough gold around his neck to make the payment on a Chevrolet Suburban. He's like a four-foot- eight-inch Mafia don.

And every girl in the room is crazy about him.

His grade point average is about a 1.0, but to these freshman girls, he is a god. They baby him, mother him, lie for him, cover for him, and do his schoolwork for him. Women's lib has not reached their neighborhood.

She doesn't get it. All this little twerp has to do is snap his fingers and these girls jump to do his bidding. Apparently bad taste starts young. The boys worship him, too, because he gets the girls.

She thinks he's either hung over every day or on drugs. He puts his head down and is sound asleep immediately. When she wakes him up (every day) he says he doesn't feel good and needs to call home and have someone bring him some medicine. She doesn't know how he manages that, though, because she's left messages at his house every day for a week and no one returns her calls.

In the beginning, Roberto and Ms. Gilbert struggled for a bit to see who was actually going to be in charge of this class. She won. But he fought the valiant fight, and now the rest of the class thinks they are punishing her for dethroning their king by not doing their class work.

She is irrelevant to them. She's this grown-up person who nags at them to pay attention, but the fact is that she just doesn't have anything to offer that's as titillating as the sex, drugs, and rap n' roll that goes on in their lives once they leave this building.

If this were a movie she would be the hero and change the lives of every one of these kids.

She would be Sidney Poitier in *To Sir, With Love.*

She would be Michelle Pfeiffer in *Dangerous Minds.*

She would be Richard Dreyfuss in *Mr. Holland's Opus.*

In reality, she's just an ordinary teacher. She wants to light the fire of curiosity in their eyes, but she can't even find the matches.

She feels like she's tried everything, but in the fifty-five minutes that she has with them each day, she can't change a lifetime of habits learned at home.

They're all miffed because they think she's picking on their precious Roberto. They've known him longer, they like him better, and he doesn't give them homework.

It's sad, but she doesn't know if she can turn it around. She thinks she's going to have to let this one go. In movies teachers always end up doing miraculous things with boys like this. But this is not a movie.

And she is not a hero.

Sometimes you just have to let the Robertos of the class put their heads down and go to sleep.

Then you can concentrate on the ones who are awake.

GETTING SKUNKED

"You have to help me. I don't know what to do. I can't teach. My students can't concentrate. This is the most embarrassing, disruptive thing that's ever happened in my classroom. Please, please, PLEASE, tell me what to do!"

That's the plea of a third year teacher.

The disruption, it seems, is caused by a windy young man who makes a daily stink in class, leaving mayhem and methane in his wake.

The teacher is convinced that this eighth grader's acoustical art is intentional.

And it probably is.

Most kids raised in polite company eventually grow out of the pull-my-finger stage. Sometimes they don't.

Other kids' reactions to such gastronomical percussion vary. Raised eyebrows, shocked scowls, silly smirks, and covered noses are typical, yet someone nearly always yells, "Oh gawd, *who cut one*?!"

And of course, faster than you can say bull snort, everyone knows who did.

Getting control of the giggling fits isn't easy. Eventually, though, it stops being funny and all eyes turn to teacher, for discipline, for solutions, for mercy.

Pressure is high. If you try to ignore it the kids will call you on it.

"Ms. Flynn," they'll whine, acutely, profoundly aggrieved. "I can't sit here. I'm getting a headache. It *smells.*"

And though the kids are perfectly willing to play musical chairs all day, the lesson plan is vaporized. And besides, the teacher can't embarrass the little gurglemeister by isolating him. Even if he embarrasses himself.

She can discreetly offer him a bathroom pass, which may or may not help. She can try talking to him, too. But really, what can she say?

"Johnny, please stop doing that."

"Doing what?"

For the refined teacher it's tough to even verbalize the problem. What words does she use to tell a parent that their child is breaking the sound barrier with enough power to launch the space shuttle? How does she say that the emissions are foul enough to disrupt class and accelerate global warming?

But call the parent she must. After all, perhaps a simple dietary adjustment will solve the problem. Then again, the call could backfire. If the parents take offense they'll be more than happy to shoot the messenger.

Can you punish a child for a natural bodily function? Can you prove they're doing it on purpose?

It's easy to tell this teacher not to sweat the small stuff. After all, there's much more serious drama unfolding in the world right now. A global financial crisis, an expensive war, and high unemployment make this little problem seem like just so much hot air.

But to the teacher and students trapped in Room 102 it's not small stuff.

They're facing weapons of class destruction.

STATE OF MIND

Mr. Wolfe has his back to the class, writing an algebra problem on the board. Cathy watches him, then takes a quick look out of the corner of her eye and sees Melinda staring at her. Their eyes lock and Melinda draws her index finger across her neck in a throat-slitting gesture, narrows her eyes, and points her finger at Cathy. Terrified, Cathy looks away. Is she going to get jumped after school?

In English class, the students are working in groups to review their five paragraph essays. Jennifer and Ashley, however, are whispering and glancing at Tabitha, giggling and rolling their eyes. Tabitha hears the word "fat" and sinks lower in her seat, certain they are talking about her. She looks down and sees that her skirt puffs out a little in front. Self-consciously, she tries to flatten it with her hand. She'll never wear this skirt again.

Jason goes to history class right after lunch. He's supposed to be reading chapter twenty-four, but all he can think about is his iPod. It was stolen at lunch and he thinks he knows who took it. It was that stoner kid, Duane, he's sure of it. He sneaks his hand into his pocket to text his buddies (a one-handed skill he has worked hard to perfect) and tells them to meet him in the alcove after school. They're going to follow the stoner home and get the iPod back. Whatever it takes.

After spending hours preparing the perfect lesson plan, teachers would like to believe that those lessons are compelling and every student is riveted. But the fact of the matter is that students don't live in an academic vacuum. By nature they're programmed to have an intense, all-consuming interest in their social and emotional growth.

And for teens and tweens it's all about the clique.

Remember cliques? Those pseudo-friendly peer networks that use inclusion, exclusion and arbitrary measures of popularity to make kids miserable?

For a student on the inside of a clique, life is good. They're assured friends to sit with at lunch, talk to in the hall, and text after school. It's wonderful to be wanted.

But for the kids who are on the outside looking in, school is a minefield of social gaffes. And cliques can turn ugly in an instant. It is unbelievable how consuming such drama can be to the students involved, and to what extent the learning environment is disrupted.

It's so easy for adults to say, "Don't worry about those kids right now. You just focus on your schoolwork." But for the outcast student struggling to learn the ways of the social world, that's about as easy as turning down a hot french fry.

This fascination with cliques includes a preoccupation with peer pressure and popularity. And when it comes to cliques, peer pressure, and popularity, teens are riddled with ambivalence.

If asked, they adamantly maintain that they don't care about such things. Yet they can rattle off the name of every clique, its subgroups, who belongs to which, and the relative merits of each (popular, preps, jocks, druggies, brains, artists, stoners, slackers, skaters, freaks, geeks, Goths, gangstas, nerds, wannabes—the list is endless and changes daily).

This is real life, and this is what the people in charge of education reform never take into consideration with their testing, numbering, labeling, measuring, and quantifying of students.

Kids are human. What's more, they're humans who happen to be going through one of the most intense, turbulent, traumatic periods of their lives. Social growth is considerable in grade school, but in junior high and high school, it is consuming.

Teachers understand the toll the social side of learning takes on the book-learning side. They struggle every day to focus kids who are preoccupied with every sort of drama and emotional upheaval, from the silly to the serious.

In the weeks leading up to homecoming or prom, for example, teens are obsessed with the dance: Will they be asked? Should they do the asking? How humiliating will it be to go alone? What will they wear? It's all they think about, all they talk about.

A dirty look—real or imagined—can preoccupy a student's mind to the exclusion of all else. Fickle friends, a zit on the chin, a bad-hair day, clumsiness in gym class, the wrong clothes, feeling too skinny or too fat—there's no end to the things students worry about.

Friends and relationships are everything. Bickering, he-said she-said, gossip, backstabbing, making up—it's all infinitely more absorbing than what the teacher has to say. And the term "drama queen" is apt: Some kids spend their days perpetually on the verge of hysterics.

Teachers walk a fine line. Just how seriously should they take such drama, when they know from experience that it will all be different next week? Just how much consolation can they give without getting sucked in and becoming part of the story? And to what extent is it all simply a need for attention?

For someone who doesn't work with kids on a daily basis, it's easy to underestimate the power of the social lives of students. When policy makers talk about educating our nation's youth, they rarely consider the whole child. For their intents and purposes, education is about instruction, drill, quizzes, tests, scores, essays, assignments, and results.

But for kids in the clutches of discovering themselves, there are far more pressing concerns.

GRIT AND FORTITUDE

"I'm not very good at writing," Jeremy said. "That's why I took this class."

OK, that might not sound particularly revelatory to most people, but to a teacher it is. Coming from a tenth grader, it's stunning.

The student in question has a learning disability that puts his writing at about the fourth grade level. The class in question is Mr. Moore's Advanced Journalism class, a demanding, fast-paced writing course that requires every student to research and write under deadline, for publication.

For the most part, high school students don't choose the difficult route no matter how much it might help them. For that matter, few people do. Most people prefer to dwell in the comfort of what they're good at, and avoid what makes them uncomfortable.

Think for a moment about the thing you struggle with. Math? Spelling? Staying organized? Nearly everyone struggles with at least one thing, something that makes their head feel as explosive as a Mentos and Diet Coke experiment.

That's what's so impressive about Jeremy. He knows the medicine is going to taste bad, but he takes it anyway.

And it does taste bad. He struggles. He is slow. The words just don't line up on the page the way they should. He toils over the most rudimentary of sentences.

Mr. Moore always lets Jeremy choose the easiest writing assignments, short, straight news stories that entail simple research. Still, he sweats over those eight or ten sentences every time. And though Mr. Moore is a pretty tough taskmaster, Jeremy stoically completes as many drafts as necessary and meets every deadline.

Because the class produces a student publication, there's no place for Jeremy to hide. His writing can't be a private matter between student and teacher. In this class, he has to put it out there for everyone to see.

Politicians and policy makers seem to think that all kids are as determined as Jeremy. That's why so much of their education legislation is ineffective. But the truth is, Jeremy is a rare gem. Far too often, even the most skilled students skate by doing the bare minimum, taking the easiest way out.

Was Jeremy simply born with an abundance of grit and fortitude? Or did his parents raise him to be that way? He certainly had every right to take a much easier class, and chose not to.

Hopefully, Jeremy will continue to approach life head-on, matter-of-factly moving forward into that which makes him stretch and grow.

Teachers use all kinds of motivational tools. But ultimately, the most authentic motivation comes from within.

CUPID CRAZY

It's a day of high spirits and higher anxiety, of feigned disinterest and heartfelt longing, of impetuous overtures and gossip gone wild.

It's Valentine's Day in a high school, and when true love hangs in the balance the lesson plan is about as interesting as the mating habits of gnats.

It is a day when teenagers yearn: for attention, validation, affection, devotion. Having recently entered the tantalizing world of the birds and the bees, their fascination with the opposite sex is perhaps more powerful now than it will ever be.

And mercy, is it powerful. Kids walk through the halls on high alert, watching waiting, anticipating, heady with the scent of Red Hots, candy conversation hearts, and cheap chocolate.

The goal on this day is to be acknowledged by someone, anyone, and a lucky few will have more than one admirer. And though not one single student will admit it, it's better to get something from someone you don't like than to get nothing at all.

The staple of the day is the single red rose, purchased on the way to school at the convenience store on the corner. By the end of the day that rose is limp with fatigue, bruised and battered, having been sniffed until the petals fall off.

Teens carry their goods like badges of honor, from balloons bumping along behind them in the halls to candy, cards, and stuffed animals piled on desks. It's as important to be seen with the spoils of love as it is to receive them.

That irresistible urge to text is stronger than ever today as kids eagerly share what they got, what they're giving, what they saw. The flip side of this love fest, of course, is the hurt feelings, rumors, and fights that erupt over slights real and imagined.

On this day school rules are bent and disruption reigns. Even the office staff is wearied by the onslaught. Floral arrangements and balloons crowd the counter until office personnel sigh in resignation. Finally, student schedules are pulled and runners dispatched to make deliveries to classrooms.

If teens are love-struck on this day, their teachers are awestruck, by lapsed attention spans and kids wound tighter than Cupid's bow string.

By the end of the day, teachers roll their eyes heavenward, impatient with the drama, the nonsense, the distractions, the endless knocks on the class-room door.

High school students are too old for Valentine's Day activities in the classroom, but matters of the heart still rule.

To keep students on task is no small thing. To keep them on task on Valentine's Day is harder than finding the caramel in a heart-shaped box of chocolates.

TRASHING THE BATHROOM

The journalism teacher answered the classroom phone and the principal said, "Do you have a student photographer available down there?" To the school newspaper adviser, the question wasn't unusual. The assignment, however, turned out to be anything but usual.

"Sure," he replied. "What's up?"

"Just send them down," he said. "Tell them to hurry."

An appalled student photographer returned fifteen minutes later. "I can't believe it," he said. "I had to take a picture of poop!"

Yep, a phantom duker had been hitting the boys' bathroom regularly, leaving his calling card in the middle of the floor. Administrators and custo-dians were at their wits' end. The photo was evidence: for what, it's hard to say.

Apologies for the inelegance of that true story. But in all honesty, some-times school is as strange as Alice's looking glass, mirroring the curiosities of the society we've created. Every single teacher has stories of the bizarre but true.

In many schools, the number one student complaint (seconded by the quality of the school lunch) is the state of the student bathrooms. Clogged sinks and toilets, empty soap dispensers, and no TP or paper towels top the list—on a good day.

On a bad day, it's beyond imagining. Vandalism. Graffiti. Destruction. One enterprising young student reporter decided to do an investigative piece on the bathroom's cleanliness. She created a checklist and visited each school bathroom four times a day, documenting what she found.

It was revolting.

Some of the mess was accidental. Most was intentional. For example, the same thick squirt of salad dressing, from a packet pilfered from the cafeteria, stayed on a stall door for four days.

It's a complex problem. The bad apples trash the bathrooms, ruining them for everybody. Heroic custodians, fed up with mopping up soap that has been intentionally poured on the floor four days in a row, eventually quit filling the soap dispensers. If the paper towel continues to be stuffed into toilets, they quit stocking those, too. If things get really bad, principals order the least patrolled bathrooms locked.

Hall monitors do their best, but they can't be everywhere at once. When students badly outnumber the adults, it's easy to find places to act out, in defiance, in anger, in ignorance.

Let's be clear about this: No school is exempt from student bathroom problems, no matter how nice the district. But the state of the student bathroom does seem to reflect the state of mind of the students who use it. What do you see driving down the street in certain parts of town?

Vandalism. Graffiti. Destruction.

In California, students protested the quality of the bathrooms, resulting in state legislation requiring schools to maintain them.

Bathroom legislation? Talk about the curiosities of society. Wouldn't it be more effective if parents simply taught their kids better bathroom etiquette?

It lends a whole new meaning to the term "potty training."

THE WICKED WEEK OF CANDY

If the incessant crinkling of wrappers doesn't make a teacher crazy, the frenzy of the sugar-buzzed beasts will.

Yes, the wicked week of candy is frightful, the week when kids' backpacks bulge not with schoolbooks, but with Halloween loot brought to school to share with some and torture others.

First, teachers must survive Halloween and the delirious glee caused by costumes and trick-or-treat anticipation. But when Halloween is over, there's a new demon to deal with: the all-consuming preoccupation with candy that is sneaked into the classroom.

Picture it: The class settles down and the lesson begins. Students listen, rapt. Suddenly, the quiet is disrupted.

Crinklecrinklecrinkle.

It's the unmistakable sound of a candy wrapper (a sound, by the way, that can rouse a dog out of a sound sleep in another room). The teacher looks around for the culprit. So does everyone else. They want to know who's got what and, more importantly, will they share? As the teacher looks pointedly around the room, the candy sneaker freezes. The crinkling stops. The lesson continues.

Soon, *crinklecrinklecrinkle.*

The teacher pretends not to hear it.

Crinklecrinklecrinkle.

Ah ha! The teacher spots her. Jennifer in the third row has a jumbo-sized bag of Skittles, a candy of such undiluted sugar quality it's like a saccharine IV. Watching kids eat one after another makes a teacher's fillings ache.

It's amazing. The sneaking of candy commands their attention, completely and utterly. The ones who brought candy are preoccupied with sneaking it out of their backpacks and into their mouths. The ones who didn't bring candy are preoccupied, too, watching the ones who did. It's as if world treaties are at stake the way the haves negotiate with the have-nots.

And so it continues, every hour, every day, until all the candy is gone.

It's annoying beyond belief.

Every teacher is tempted to give into it, to say, "Oh, what the heck. Go ahead, eat your candy. Eat it until your teeth fall out!"

Visualize thirty kids corked up on sugar and fortunately, reason returns.

The coup de grace is that wrappers from the candy you never saw them eat are all over the classroom floor when they leave.

Crinklecrinklecrinkle.

Mmmm. . . a Snickers mini.

If you can't beat'em, join'em.

THE BLACK HOLE

He jumped up next to his desk when the bell rang, all eighty-eight knock-kneed pounds of him. He hefted the brand new backpack filled with twenty-five pounds of just-issued textbooks, slung it over his shoulder. . . and. . . the laws of physics kicked in. Weight and momentum carried the pack to the other side of his seat and, like a slow motion cartoon, pulled that poor, astonished freshman to the ground, eyes wide, feet in the air. The backpack landed on the floor with a thud, with him still attached to it.

Turtled.

Ah yes, the backpack. It's a keeper of secrets, desktop pillow, personal billboard and grade detonator, as its disorganized contents are often the cause of student failure.

High school—especially big high schools—can be an unsettling adjustment after the relative comfort of junior high. Lockers can be far from classes and passing time is short; too short if you ask the kids, who live for those five minutes of bliss, hanging with friends, sneaking text time and updating their Facebook status. But it's plenty long if you ask the principals who watch the kids hang with friends and sneak cell phone calls, then rush late to class.

Thus, into the backpack everything goes so no time is wasted stopping at a locker. Parents who brave a peek into the backpack might be surprised by what they find. In addition to the textbooks, iPod, energy drink, candy wrappers, smart phone, and smelly gym shirt, there's a wad of paper hard and heavy enough to use as a doorstop, as assignments and handouts get shoved in on top of each other, never making it into the folders that that were so earnestly bought at the beginning of the year. Over time those papers mold together into amazing, abstract, sculpturesque works of art.

Hour after hour, day after day, week after week, papers are shoved in and promptly forgotten. That assignment he worked on last night that never got turned in? Still in the backpack. The permission slip he said he lost? Still in the backpack. Instructions for the big marking period project in history? Still in the backpack. The interim report you never saw? Yep, sucked into the black hole of the backpack.

For freshmen, lack of organization contributes to their failure as much as anything else.

And while the backpack seems to hold the very lifeblood of a student, kids can be surprisingly blasé about them, too. Just check any school's lost and found and there sit half a dozen abandoned bulging backpacks, never to be claimed by fickle owners who simply purchase another one and move on.

Oh, and the turtled freshman? Well, by the end of the year he had grown into his backpack.

All that weight lifting, no doubt.

A MOMENT IN THE SUN

". . . So when you turn in your end-of-year project, please make sure to. . ."
ERT. ERT. ERT. ERT. ERT. ERT. ERT. ERT.
Suddenly, the mechanical, ear-piercing sound of the fire alarm shatters the quiet, jolting students into alertness, jerking them upright in their seats.

Yes, it's that time of year, when the weather turns warm and schools squeeze in the last of their state mandated fire drills. And though their timing might be unpredictable for students and teachers, the weather on this day is not, as administrators nearly always schedule them for the first gorgeous day in spring.

As students bolt from their seats and scramble for the door, teachers try to give instructions over the noise, every other word drowned out by the din. They grab attendance books and grade books, close windows, lock doors, then hustle to catch up with their students.

Hurrying through the halls they pass directly under the fire alarms mounted high on the walls. The blast is earsplitting and reflexively hands shoot up to cover ears, protecting them from the sound. Strident and unrelenting, it's like a test of the emergency broadcast system on television or radio, but echoing in the enclosed hallway it is ten, twenty, fifty times louder.

Teachers take turns holding the doors as kids stream through, then scurry to look for their own. Students are supposed to stay with their class, but it's like trying to corral a litter of puppies.

It's a blessed relief to get outside, away from the deafening noise. Relief from the blast is immediately replaced by sudden pain from blinding light as they step out into the brilliant spring sun. Now hands reflexively shoot up to shield eyes more accustomed to artificial light. Bumping along like a slow-moving herd, everyone squints and blinks, struggling to adjust.

Once outside kids gleefully dissolve into the crowd. Then they scatter to find friends from other classes, while teachers do their best to round them up. It's an impossible task and they soon give up, and settle for watching the perimeter of the group, making sure no one wanders away.

The day is dazzling. Some chat with friends, but others simply stand in the sweet-smelling dandelion grass, dazed with pleasure, faces tipped toward the sun, soaking up blue sky and clean fresh air.

When the all-clear bell rings the mob turns like sheep and heads back in, infinitely more slowly, less enthusiastically, than they headed out.

Teachers reach their classrooms first and wait impatiently for stragglers, eager to get back to the lesson, back to the routine of year-end assignments.

Projects, papers, portfolios, tests. It's a mad race to the end of the school year.

But oh, what a delicious treat are those few unexpected moments in the sun.

Blackboard Jungle Bells
(Sung to the tune of "Jingle Bells")

Dashing through the halls, through the pre-vacation fray
Kids racing to and fro, laughing all the way;
The noise makes my head throb, My God, I look a fright
What toil it is to tame the beasts, this day to expedite
(Chorus)
Starting bells, tardy bells, ring in the hallway!
O what grit one has to have to make it through this day
Sugar high, caffeine buzz, what more can I say?
O what fun winter break will be, let's hear a big hooray!

Of course it had to snow, and complicate my plight
I slipped and fell right on my tush much to the kids' delight
Snowballs flying fast, shoes and coats all wet
Kids caught up in being kids, gone is all etiquette
(Chorus)
A day or two ago, so close to this Yuletide
The whole class had a cold, sniffling and red-eyed.
The Kleenex box ran dry, but Johnny's nose did not.
He got into a sneezing fit, and slimed my sleeve with snot
(Chorus)
The kids just can't sit still, they know vacation's near
Lessons are a bore to them this special time of year
But teachers must push on, learning's the bottom line
The struggle has exhausted me and it's only half past nine
(Chorus)
The lunch buffet was grand. Someone tried it all,
They pushed it to the max, now there's vomit in the hall.
The kids don't seem to mind, they all got quite a laugh,
The culprit was Mr. McGraw, a teacher on the staff
(Chorus)
The kids have all pitched in, raised money for the poor
You only have to watch them work to have your faith restored
Gifts for a lonely child, and food for those in need
In spite of what you generally hear their motive is not greed
(Chorus)
Last hour's finally here, one more to make it through
My feet and back do ache, but I'm not sad or blue
The giggling smiles of kids, sustained me all day long
They've piled my desk with candy canes, and courted me with song
(Chorus)
At last the day is done, the kids burst forth with glee
They race from the classroom, I dodge the stampede;
I flop down at my desk, and realize the truth
One reason that I love to teach: The enthusiasm of youth!
(Chorus)

AS OUTDATED AS ENGLISH MONARCHY

She's pretty, she's sweet, and although she doesn't know it, she's hopelessly out of style.

She is the homecoming queen.

High schools, ironically, institutions that strive to promote equality and be politically correct, continue to support a contest that objectifies girls almost as much as a bad music video.

Years ago, when the idea of homecoming queen was conceived, women had very different roles. Their worth was judged on their looks and the mate they won. Once married, they were judged on their cooking and the cleanliness of the house they kept.

But it's the twenty-first century and schools still cling to an obsolete measure of a girl. It's way past time that our daughters aspire to something more than a popularity contest.

Girls should be taught to have a sense of accomplishment that comes from within, rather than from without. They need to know that they're special and powerful because of what they can do, not how they look. We should expose girls to experiences that empower them, where they are judged on their accomplishments rather than promote an archaic contest where their sense of self-worth is bestowed by their peers.

In a weak attempt at equality, some schools have adopted a king contest, completely missing the point. Adding a king doesn't change the fact that contests for queen are fluff and fiction. After all, what, exactly does the homecoming queen excel at? Usually, at fitting in.

Unfortunately, the damage isn't only done to the queen and her court. Every other girl who wishes she was on that court gets the wrong message too, as does every boy who votes. One silly contest dims the confidence of every girl who doesn't make the cut.

The very fact that we spend so much time and money on the homecoming queen contest tells students that it's important. Class is disrupted for assemblies and voting, it gets its own spread in the yearbook, and it's covered by the media, sending the message that we'll pull out all the stops for the pretty, popular girls.

Let's raise girls who are comfortable in their own skin. Let's raise girls who want to be measured by their creativity, kindness, skills, compassion, talent, leadership, bravery, and civic-mindedness. Let's teach girls to recognize homecoming queen contests for the shallow aspirations they are.

It's possible that many district officials would be happy to be rid of the headache of the homecoming queen contest, but no one wants to be first. It's hard to change a long-standing tradition, even when it's wrong. If one school district challenges it though, the rest will follow.

It's not that these girls aren't talented. It's just that this disempowering contest is never about talent. And it's not that homecoming should be abolished. It's a week filled with fun activities that build school spirit.

But the tradition of homecoming queen is obsolete. Every thinking adult knows it.

Our girls just don't know it.

And they won't unless we tell them.

BOYS GONE BAD

At first it just seemed like ordinary jostling in the crowded school halls. Four boys, walking elbow to elbow in a tight row, came up close behind her, almost stepping on her heels.

Suddenly she felt a hand reach around and cup her breast. Another hand grabbed her bottom and squeezed, hard. She gasped in fright and embarrassment, but was so tightly packed in by the crowd that she couldn't move away.

Whirling around, she came face to face with the laughing jeers of the four boys. Their hands were now in their pockets.

"Don't touch me!" she hissed.

"What?" the boys asked, eyes wide in feigned innocence. "What are you talking about?"

School principals across the country deal with variations of that scene far too often. It's a growing problem, and one of the most frustrating and time-consuming things principals face.

The parent of a middle school child described the same thing in a letter to the syndicated advice column, "Annie's Mailbox." The letter writer expressed outrage that administrators at her daughter's school didn't put a stop to it.

The parent's outrage is understandable. But for administrators, the answers don't come easy.

It's not that perplexed school administrators aren't trying to stop it. But the boys are sly. They know that by traveling in a pack they make it difficult for the girl to identify which of them actually touched her. They're savvy enough to know that, even if guilty, they have as many rights as the victim.

And then they simply deny it. They know that without a witness, administrators have to be very careful about unjustly accusing the wrong person. Because while the girls' parents fiercely protect their daughters, the boys' parents just as fiercely protect their sons. After all, no parent wants to believe that their son is grabbing girls' breasts in public.

How do boys get away with this? Well, in today's super-sized schools where the students greatly outnumber the adults, it's easy for kids to find long stretches of unsupervised hallway. Just like at home, kids know where the adults are.

And where they aren't.

So what's a principal to do? First they'll bring the boys into their office one at a time and question them. They might even bring in another principal or a liaison police officer and play good cop, bad cop. They'll try to catch the boys off guard and find inconsistencies in their stories. They'll question other students if they can. Several hours out of the principal's day may be consumed with one incident. If the boys stick to their stories, though, there's not much more a principal can do.

Gone are the days when a boy who got fresh would get a swift, hard slap across the face from a girl. Today, that same slap may cause a girl to be suspended from school, or worse, charged with assault.

Girls are encouraged to speak up, not suffer in silence, to get help from an adult. And some do. But for every girl who speaks up, how many more are afraid to for fear of retribution from the boys? After all, if the boys think little enough of them to violate them like this in the first place, what would they do to a girl who squealed?

The crux of the matter is, why do the boys think this is okay? Might it have something to do with the music they listen to and the video games they play, where girls are objectified and called bitches, sluts, and ho's? Might it be because their role models are based on celebrity, not character?

Much of the solution focuses on the girls, telling them to be brave and point fingers and name names. That's a start, but it doesn't put the onus where it belongs.

Don't assume that your son knows better. If you haven't talked to him about the proper way to treat a girl, who has?

THE MOST WONDERFUL DAY OF THE YEAR

"Na na na na, Na na na na, Hey hey hey, Goodbye. Na na na na, Na na na na, Hey seniors, Goodbye."

She stands in the doorway of her classroom watching the senior class walk arm in arm down the hall, singing. She clenches her teeth to keep from blubbering, but when she looks over at the teacher in the next doorway, she's wiping her eyes, too.

And why shouldn't they cry like sentimental fools? After all, this is what it's all about for teachers, the reward of their life's work. Thirteen years of education culminate in this celebration. They're proud. Happy. Gratified.

And wary. After all, anything can happen on this, the seniors' last day of school. Pumped, manic, intoxicated with nostalgia, the students fairly throb with emotion. They've been threatened with everything teachers can think of, including not walking down the aisle at graduation, to keep them from doing something stupid today.

It starts at 5:30 a.m., when seniors, most of whom were hard-pressed all year to drag themselves out of bed and get to school on time, arrive in the student parking lot. They make banners and signs, paint their faces and clothes, and enter the building arm-in-arm, singing joyfully, tearfully, just before the first bell.

Security is on the scene early, as well, and principals and hall monitors and teachers. Not interfering. Just watching. Just in case.

Because for staff, until that last bell rings at 2:30, it's all about containment.

Undergrads bounce off the walls, too, caught up in the excitement. Little real teaching will happen today. Some teachers give tests in an effort to keep students focused. Others have parties, adding to the hysteria by way of sugar-high. Missed deadlines caused by acute senioritis require many kids to spend the day completing projects, slap-dashing them together, racing to turn them in.

It's an all-day hug-fest, kids suddenly clinging to people they've never even talked to. Camcorders record every last smile, cameras flash endlessly, memory books are passed around and signed.

Some students, unfortunately, spend the day cajoling, bribing, and flat-out begging teachers to pass them, in spite of having had multiple warnings of impending failure. It's heartbreaking for teachers to deny them. Tears over leaving good friends mingle with tears over poor grades and failure.

It's a thrilling, demanding, exhausting day, and when that last bell rings, teachers roll their eyes heavenward and say a little prayer of thanks. Whoops and hollers echo as kids pour out of the building. When the last car squeals out of the parking lot, teachers at last breathe easily. The sudden hush is blissful.

They've done their part. The seniors are finally gone, and teachers are glad to see them go. But it's relief mixed with apprehension. After all, for seniors, the celebrating has just begun.

No longer under our protective wing, they're off doing God knows what, God knows where.

Chapter Three

Parents

From absenteeism and grade inflation to prom paparazzi and the X-rated boogie

Parents often talk about the younger generation as if they didn't have anything to do with it.

—Dr. Haim Ginott

ADVOCATE, DON'T DEPRECATE

If you don't like the way your child's teacher does something, say so.

If you want to know why she does things a certain way, ask.

If you have a suggestion, share it.

Make no mistake, it is your duty—and your right—to be involved in your child's education. And as you and your child get acquainted with a new teacher, you'll no doubt have questions or concerns about policies and procedures.

It could be anything: discipline, snack time, reading groups, birthdays, recess, seating charts, homework, makeup work, assignments, tests. The scope of parental concerns is huge.

And that's okay. If you have questions or doubts about anything that's happening in your child's classroom it's your job to look into it.

So call the teacher. Send an e-mail. Write a letter. Make an appointment. State your case. Be specific. Say exactly what's on your mind, and what you'd like to see done differently. Then listen. Work the lines of communication. Brainstorm. Share ideas. Be open to suggestions.

Speak up. Get involved. Ask questions.

But whatever you do, *don't let your child know about it.*

You can be your child's advocate in dozens of ways, but keep it between you and the teacher. Because the minute your child senses that you have an unfavorable feeling toward their teacher, that you dislike them or don't respect them, your child will start to feel the same way. And once that happens, you have negatively influenced your child's feelings about that class. Those negative feelings will spill over into other classes, and other schools.

You will alter your child's attitude toward education forever.

And what's worse, your feelings and behavior will infect other students, as well. If your child tells other kids about your complaints, you have just changed the learning environment in that classroom for every single student.

This is not melodrama. Every day, all over the country, for countless reasons, parents race to school in a snit about one thing or another and make a scene. The cumulative effect of unprofessional parental meddling has soured thousands of kids on the educational experience.

Sadly, too many parents confuse the intensity of their advocacy with the intensity of their love for their child.

But if you really want to show how much you love your child, teach them to revere learning and to respect the educational process, even if you don't agree with it 100 percent. No matter what school they attend or which teacher they have, they will be far better off with a positive attitude toward learning.

You owe it to your child to participate in his education. You can ask all the questions you want.

But work behind the scenes. Not center stage.

PARENTS PEGGED AT CONFERENCES

When parents sit down across the desk at parent/teacher conferences, everything that teacher has ever wondered about a kid suddenly becomes crystal clear. Talk about a learning experience. . .

The Bully

This parent bullies the student right in front of the teacher, demanding that the student account for the grade. Their belligerence is unsettling. The student often lies about why the grade is so low and the teacher is left to decide how much to rat on the kid. They can tell all, or help the kid out and hold something back. Sometimes if they hold something back the kid is grateful and will make an effort to do better next time. When parent and child finally leave, the teacher wonders and worries: what happened when they got home?

The Three-Ring Circus

This parent makes a big show of being tough with the kid, the kid argues back, and neither of them listens to a word the teacher says. The parent asks a question, the teacher starts to answer, the kid interrupts and makes excuses about his grade. Pretty soon the kid has successfully diverted the parents' attention and they're off, arguing about everything. The teacher watches for a while and then they leave. The teacher feels slightly used after an encounter like this, as if he's merely been a prop in the drama.

The Perfectionist

The perfectionist grills the teacher about why the child got an A-. Sometimes these parents ask the teacher to tutor their child after school. They shake their heads, wrinkle their brow, and mutter under their breath that an A- is not acceptable. It's hard to know if they are upset with the teacher, or the child, but that A- almost always gets raised to an A.

The Shy

The shy parent comes in, sits down, and squirms uncomfortably. The teacher tells them a little bit about the class, the work, their child's performance, and then asks if they have any questions. They usually don't. It's as if they are there because they think they should be, as if they read it in a parenting handbook but didn't quite understand the chapter. They don't know when to leave and quietly wait to be dismissed.

The Blamers

These parents blame everything and everybody except their own child for the child's performance. They grill the teacher, looking for a loophole, a chink in his armor, a weakness in his teaching methods or grading system, something, anything, they can pounce on. Teachers learn quickly not to volunteer information and to keep their answers short. The teacher must keep his voice neutral and his face expressionless, lest they take offense to his tone or manner. These are the parents that teach teachers the importance of keeping scrupulous notes, to save his hide if he finds himself in court. The teacher sprints and dodges as fast as a quarterback when he sees these parents in public, even ducking behind a display of socks at Target to hide.

The Apathetic

This is the apathetic girl and her bewildered mother:

Mother: (*plaintive*) I don't know why Susie has such a low grade. She never brings any homework home.

Teacher: Well, Susie didn't complete twelve assignments, and these weren't even homework, they were done in class.

Mother: (*turns to daughter, clearly perplexed*). Why didn't you turn them in?

Susie: (*sullen, won't meet mother's eyes, or the teacher's, shrugs*)

Mother: Susie, why don't you do the assignments if you have plenty of time in class?

Susie: (*shrugs again, turns head away, looks bored, stares off into space*)

Mother: (*looks to teacher for help*)

Teacher: Susie, why don't you do the work?

Susie: (*shrugs again, squirms a little*)

Teacher: Is the work too difficult for you?

Susie: No.

Teacher: I don't think it is either. You're a bright girl and you should be acing this class.

Susie:

Mother nags a little more, daughter refuses to respond, rolls her eyes a few times, looks like she can't stand her mother. (At this point, neither can the teacher.) Mother gives up easily, states several times that she doesn't know what to do, and eventually the apathetic pair wanders off.

The Supportive

Supportive parents are surprisingly few and far between, but they are a breath of fresh air. These are the parents who are interested in the curriculum, interested to know what their child's strengths and weaknesses are, and who are supportive of the teacher and the school system. These are the parents that teachers keep in touch with after their child has graduated, parents that they're happy to run into at the grocery store or the mall. These parents love their kids unconditionally, but are savvy enough to know that kids will be kids and even theirs aren't perfect. They take this with a grain of salt and a sense of humor. They keep an open mind and know that by treating teachers with respect, they teach their children the most important lesson of all: to value education.

CAN YOU HANDLE THE TRUTH?

Do you know what your teenager is up to?

Are you sure?

American lifestyles have changed in the last few decades. Kids are afforded more privacy than ever, and that's not necessarily a good thing. Think back a few decades: Houses used to be smaller and families were larger, making it hard to hide anything from anybody. Homes had one bathroom, shared by all. Everyone shared one phone, too, which usually hung on the wall in the kitchen. For privacy, the phone cord was stretched around the corner as far as it would go. Families had one television, in the living room, and everyone shared it. Dinner was served once, and everyone ate together.

In many families today, the exact opposite is true. Kids have cell phones, televisions and computers, even mini-fridges in their bedrooms, and often a private bath. Dinner is eaten at different times, in different parts of the house. And many family members don't even see each other every day. The result is that most kids have a great deal of unsupervised private time.

But there's another, more alarming reason that parents don't know what their teenagers are up to.

They don't want to know.

Parents may acknowledge that teens do drugs and have sex, but they don't believe that their kids do drugs and have sex.

But it's not just parents who are letting kids down. Our culture is letting teenagers down by looking the other way, by stepping back when we should be stepping in.

Teachers hear and see a lot of what their students are up to. But they learn early in their careers to be very careful about what they tell parents because parents have no qualms about shooting the messenger when confronted with things they don't want to hear.

While teaching logarithmic function to freshmen one day, Ms. Lamott happened to intercept a note being passed from Brian to James. She tossed it into her desk drawer and continued with the lesson. Later that day, while looking for a yellow highlighter, she came across the note. As she was about to toss it into the trash, the word "ecstasy" caught her attention. She opened the note and read it, and found a detailed description of a weekend party Brian attended and the drugs he'd done while there.

Worried, Ms. Lamott went to her principal for advice. The principal told Ms. Lamott that she made a tactical error; she shouldn't have read the note. Now that she had, however, she couldn't ignore what was in it. She had to call the boy's mother.

Ms. Lamott called Brian's mom and asked her to pick up the note. Upon her arrival, the mom made it clear that having to come to the school was a huge imposition. She read the note and then huffily told Ms. Lamott she would talk to Brian about it.

The next day the mom called Ms. Lamott. She said Brian explained the whole thing and that it was all just a big misunderstanding. He didn't really use the drugs. The mom was clearly angry with Ms. Lamott for insinuating that he did. When class met again, Brian was angry, too.

Ms. Lamott continued to see and hear evidence of Brian's drug use for the rest of the year. But short of catching him red-handed, there was nothing more she could do. She never shared her concerns with his mother again.

She never read another note passed by a student again, either.

A few months later, Ms. Lamott watched as Brittany, one of her most polite and scholarly students, got pulled under the spell of an older, faster, mean girl named Melinda. Soon, Brittany started behaving badly, too. Ms. Lamott had talked with Brittany's mother at several conferences, so she called her to share her observations.

The first thing Brittany's mother wanted to know, of course, was the name of the older girl. Ms. Lamott hedged. This was dicey. But, she reasoned, how could the mom intervene if she didn't know who the bad influence was? Besides, Ms. Lamott knew that if it were her own daughter she would want to know, too. So she told her.

The mother talked with Brittany and shared Ms. Lamott's concerns. Brittany told Melinda, Melinda told her own mom, and soon Melinda's mom called, accusing Ms. Lamott of bad-mouthing her daughter.

It's a dilemma teachers face every day as they walk the line of political correctness. They know which kids are trouble, but they can't say which kids are trouble.

If a teacher sees a student in immediate danger, say physically abused or suicidal, they will, of course, follow the appropriate procedure. But there's a whole lot that teachers see that parents don't hear about.

Do your teen's teachers know more about what they're up to than you do? It's possible. Are they going to tell you? Maybe. Maybe not.

It depends on whether or not you're willing to hear it.

IN THEIR BUSINESS

Apparently Big Brother is not the only one who's watching.

Mom and Dad are watching, too.

James Bond-like surveillance equipment is now de rigueur at electronics stores, and it's being touted as a way to keep tabs on teenagers. It's also surprisingly affordable. Sadly, after years of letting television babysit kids, we now let surveillance equipment do it.

But hi-tech equipment can't take the place of a real, live parent. Teenagers need guidance. One on one. They need to know that the adults in their lives are going to be there, in their business, every time they turn around.

Fortunately, there are still many wonderful, involved parents, people who could write books on good parenting. Unfortunately, there are far too many absent parents. It's not unusual for a teacher to spend over a week trying to reach a parent by phone, even if they leave a message every single day.

If parents want to know what their kids are up to, they need to be where they are. And some savvy parents use some pretty creative, hands-on approaches.

Jason, for example, had a serious tardiness problem. He just couldn't get to class on time. His dad, bless his heart, decided that he wanted to see why Jason couldn't get to class on time, so he came to school and escorted him to all six of his classes. In spite of the fact that Dad worked nights and needed to sleep, he sat in the back of every one of Jason's classes that day, struggling to keep his eyes open.

And it worked. Jason got the message, loud and clear. If he couldn't make it to class on time, Dad was going to make it his business to know why.

Allen wouldn't pay attention in class. He was also disruptive and rude. His teacher called home and described his behavior to his father and then invited him in to see for himself.

When Allen's dad walked into that third hour class and sat down in the back row, the kids whispered and pointed. When unsuspecting Allen walked in and saw his dad sitting there, the color drained from his face.

Needless to say, Allen didn't act up that day. In fact, he didn't act up again. Just knowing that his dad might show up was enough to keep him in line.

Unbeknownst to Kevin, his dad arrived toward the end of sixth hour and waited outside the classroom for him. When the bell rang kids poured into the hall, and there was Dad waiting for Kevin. A loud conversation ensued drawing the teacher to the door to make sure everything was okay.

"What the heck is you doin' with yo' pants down 'round yo' butt like that?" the dad hollered.

"I done tol' you and tol' you, no son of mine is gon' walk 'round in public with his pants down below his butt. You get them pants, up, son, I'm telling you, right now. You don't gotta' belt, I git you some rope, but you gon' get them pants up now!"

Apparently Kevin and his dad had had this conversation before.

You want to know what your kids are up to?
Be there.

IT'S THE LITTLE THINGS

It's eight o'clock on a school night and the pub is noisy and full. When the waitress arrives, a mom at a table of eight asks her for a pencil. Her, son, she says, needs to do his homework.

The child pushes plates and glasses aside to make a little room on the table for his paper, while the adults around him laugh and talk and drink their beer. The child is drinking a Coke.

And while Mom gets points for making sure the homework is done, one has to wonder why the child is out so late on a school night, and why he's drinking caffeine at bedtime.

Ask students about their lives outside of school and you'll see that there are all sorts of seemingly inconsequential things that interfere with learning. For example, kids routinely report that they could not do their homework because they were not at home the night before. They offer this up matter-of-factly, believing themselves blameless because of it.

And perhaps they are. After all, how can they do homework if they spend the entire evening trapped in the car, being dragged to the laundromat, the bank, and half a dozen stores, visiting friends and relatives, stopping here to drop off this and there to pick up that? Sometimes it takes weeks to get ahold of a parent, leaving message after message in a house where no one is home.

Lack of sleep is a huge problem, too. A surprising number of students say they can't sleep at night, and yet they drink caffeinated beverages all day and into the evening.

These are not the children who are overscheduled in organized activities like gymnastics, soccer, and dance. This is the trivial busyness that keeps some families running all the time.

These are not bad parents. The worst that can be said is that they are, perhaps, unfocused, overbooked, and disorganized. The problem is that kids get too used to the busyness, never learn how to fill their own time, and become easily bored when there is no outside stimulus to entertain them.

Teachers are aware of dozens of such impediments to learning, seemingly insignificant, yet insidious things that are too intangible to be quantified and measured.

And because they haven't been quantified and measured, they will never be cited as a cause for bad grades or low test scores. Yet they have a profound effect on a student's performance in school.

Everyone is busier than they'd like to be. But when you look at why a student isn't performing in school, it's important to look at the whole picture.

HOMEWORK MEANS WORK AT HOME

There's so much hype about homework, it's hard to know what to believe. Too much? Too little? It depends which study is cited.

Or which parents are asked. Of course, kids don't like homework. But more and more, parents feel like it's an imposition, too. Teachers come away from parent/teacher conferences shaking their heads. Are they giving too much homework? Or not enough?

But lately there are two curious twists to the homework dilemma. The first is that many kids seem to feel that teachers have no right to give them homework. In some convoluted reasoning, being protected from homework is similar to being protected from corporal punishment or verbal abuse. They seem to think that homework is a violation of their rights. There's sort of a "You can make me do schoolwork while I'm here, but your rights don't extend into my home life" attitude.

Our litigious society has taught students to look for every loophole. The prevailing notion is that their personal time is off limits, and if they miss school they should be allowed to use class time to make up work. Variations of this conversation happen between students and teachers every day:

Johnny: (*worried, panicked*) "Teacher, it's not fair, I wasn't here yesterday, do I get extra time to work on this newspaper project?"

Teacher: (*calm, neutral*) "Yes, you may take it home and finish it and turn it in the day after tomorrow."

Johnny: "Well, I don't get the newspaper at home, so I can't."

Teacher: "I have lots of newspapers. Take as many as you need."

Johnny: "But it's not my fault I was absent. I was sick."

Teacher: "Well, whatever the reason, you still have to make up the work if you want a grade. And you can't do it in class because you'll miss what we're doing today and get further behind."

Johnny: "Well, I don't have time to do it at home!"

Teacher: (*shrugging*) "Well, that's how it works. When you're absent you have to do your makeup work at home."

Johnny: (*stomping off angrily*) *"It's not my fault I got the flu!"*

Parents don't want to hear the second truth about homework.

Kids lie.

Parents repeatedly tell teachers that their child comes home every night and says he doesn't have homework. When shown the grade book and all of the homework assignments that their child has not done, their response is plaintive: "Well, there's nothing I can do if he lies to me about it!"

During a discussion with his class about study habits, Mr. Wroblewski asked his students if their parents ever inquired about their homework. Derek, a freshman, candidly volunteered his method for getting out of it. He said that whenever his mom asked if he had his homework done, he purposely mumbled. He would turn the other way, leave the room, and mumble over his shoulder. He said it worked every time and she always let it go. He said he didn't feel bad about it because he wasn't actually lying.

Poor kid. As Derek sang like a jailbird, proudly sharing that little gem with the class, it never once occurred to him that by the time he got home, Mr. Wroblewski would have shared it with his mom, too.

PUT SOME CLOTHES ON, GIRL

You shouldn't stare, but face it, it's hard not to. High school girls are pushing dress code limits like never before.

The warm months are the true test of a high school's dress code, namely in the form of itsy-bitsy teeny-weeny clothes that not-so-itsy-bitsy teeny-weeny girls wear.

Educators don't want to deal with dress codes. They have better things to do. But if parents are going to let them out of the house like that, then they're going to get busted when they arrive.

It's not about morality. Parents have made it more than clear that they don't want public schools to teach values. And public schools have too much to do anyway.

For school personnel it's about disruption. It takes no more than a change in the wind to distract a teenager from the task at hand, especially if they aren't all that keen on the task to begin with. And the lure of a tush peeking out from under microshorts, breasts being pushed up out of tank tops, and thongs riding up out of low-riders is a big-time distraction.

Students need the freedom to express themselves. And many of the latest styles for girls are cute. But school isn't a party, and anything that distracts from the work at hand is a problem, just as it would be in the workplace.

When Mr. Koontz steps up to the podium at the beginning of his second period history class, he looks down at the front row and sees a sophomore girl wearing an extremely low-cut top. More of her chest shows than doesn't, and on her breast is a great big purple hickey.

Did you gasp?

If you haven't spent time in a high school recently you may have.

If she's brazen enough to come to school like that, then she's wearing that hickey like a badge of honor. She's not going to take kindly to being disciplined for showing it.

Of course the other kids have seen it. Of course they're talking about it, or at the very least thinking about it. How interesting is the Civil War going to be when the hottie next to you has a hickey on her breast?

Then she'll say that she wore this shirt to school before and no one said anything. And that may or may not be true. Sometimes teachers get so busy that they just don't notice what every kid in every class is wearing. Sometimes they choose not to notice. Why add more aggravation to an already aggravating day?

Referring her to the office will likely result in a showdown. She'll want to know just what, exactly, is wrong with her outfit, making the teacher explain out loud what is inappropriate. Even if he takes her into the hall to discuss it privately, chances are she'll gripe aloud to the class about the injustice of it all and they'll back her up.

Mentioning the shirt is suicide enough—but the hickey? Don't even go there. It's a no-win conversation. "It's not a hickey, it's a birthmark, and what are you doing looking there anyway (you creepy old pervert)?" she'll say.

And there you have it. One girl's inappropriate attire has just wasted ten minutes of this teacher's time and the time of every student in that class. Imagine countless variations of that story and that's what high schools deal with in the warm months. Multiply that by hundreds of kids and, you get the picture.

Three days later another girl struts into Mr. Koontz's class and flops defiantly into her chair in the front row. On her t-shirt it says, in large capital letters, "GODDESS OF FUCK."

He just shakes his head.

And hands her a pass to the office.

THE X-RATED BOOGIE

Chaperoning the prom used to be fun. The glitz, glamour, elegance, and excess of a senior prom are truly something to see. But the excess is no longer reserved for expensive gowns and huge limousines. Now, not only is the attire excessive, but the behavior is, too.

Chaperoning the prom used to be easy. One really only had to watch for the basic stuff: booze, smoking, a fight brewing, or maybe a couple making out in a dark corner. And because kids' behavior really does improve when they're dressed like grown-ups, problems were few and far between.

But in recent years, chaperoning any event that involves teenagers and music has become a behemoth battle of wills as teens pump, thump, bump, and hump to the music of their generation.

We call it dirty dancing.

They call it a generation gap.

Chaperones now spend their time patrolling the dance floor, continuously telling kids to clean it up or leave.

And sometimes the behavior is truly outrageous. Ms. Lansens, a Senior English teacher, has not missed a prom in the last twenty-nine years. She loves seeing her flock feathered in their finest, elegant and grown-up, just days before they leave the nest for good. To Ms. Lansens, prom is a rite of passage, a bridge from childhood to adulthood.

As she walks the perimeter of the dance floor, she notices about two dozen kids in a tight circle in the darkest corner, facing inward, clapping and cheering at whatever is going on in the middle. She pauses a moment to watch. It doesn't look particularly dangerous, but something in the air makes her decide to investigate further.

When she finally pushes through the crowd, it takes her a minute to process what she sees. A beautiful girl in a long white gown made of some shimmery, slinky jersey material. The dress is backless, low-cut in front, of a fabric as thin as a slip. It looks absolutely gorgeous on her long lanky frame.

The girl is bent over at the waist, hands planted firmly on her thighs, pumping her rear up and down in time to the music. Her long blond hair hangs down around her shoulders, obscuring her face from view. Against her backside, with his pelvis pressed tightly against her rear, is a young man in a tuxedo. He is holding the girl firmly by the shoulders as he, too, pumps to the music.

Ms. Lansens' heart lurches. Is the girl. . .being held there against her will? She rushes over.

"Let go of her this instant!" Ms. Lansens growls.

The boy laughs. And keeps pumping. The crowd of kids keeps clapping.

"Go, go, go!" they chant.

Ms. Lansens looks around, confused. What are they cheering for?

Suddenly she gets it. Like spectators at a sporting event, they are egging the couple on.

She moves in closer. The girl's head is still down, hair swinging from side to side.

"Stop!" Ms. Lansens commands. The boy laughs and spins off. The girl stands up, flips her hair back, and laughs, too.

"*What?*" the girl asks, exasperated.

"Are you okay?" Ms. Lansens asks.

"Uh, *yeah*," the girl says, sarcastically.

"What were you thinking then, letting that boy do that to you?" she says, frowning.

"We were *dancing*," the girl says nonchalantly.

"That was *not* dancing," Ms. Lansens replies firmly. "Would you dance like that in front of your mother?"

"My mother *taught* me," the girl says snottily, again with the hair flip.

Her mother didn't teach her that. No doubt her mother has no idea that she dances like that. In fact, most parents probably don't know how their kids dance. Because if parents are watching they're probably getting the PG version of an X-rated boogie.

When school personnel try to talk with kids about appropriate dancing at school functions, kids roll their eyes and snort. Adults are hopelessly old-fashioned, they say, they just don't get it, it doesn't mean a thing, *everyone* does it, it's just the way they dance.

To combat the issue, many schools have created guidelines for dances, stating that any action that simulates sex is taboo. Some have forbidden the DJ to play certain songs. Some have gone so far as to make kids sign a contract when they purchase their tickets, agreeing that they won't dance dirty.

The only real solution is for parents, especially dads, to get involved and attend dances. If they do, though, they'd better have the paramedics standing by.

Because they are going to be left breathless, speechless, and blinded by what they see.

TO SUSPEND . . .

"I know, I can't do anything with him at home, either."

It's hard to believe how often teachers hear those words when they call a parent to discuss a student's misbehavior in class. The subtext? "You're on your own."

And yet, in an infuriating irony, schools face derision for suspending too many rude, disruptive, violent children, whose parents consider the public school system to be nothing more than a free babysitting service.

Five minutes of the television show *Supernanny* depicts the problem precisely. A lot of parents are absolutely clueless about how to set boundaries and discipline their children.

Record numbers of parents have no control over their children, yet camouflage their parental inadequacy by pointing the finger at someone else—namely, the school system that has the gall to say, "Your bad behavior is not welcome here."

But before pointing that finger, consider this: When school personnel are forced to spend an inordinate amount of time dealing with a defiant child, they are cheating dozens of other children out of meaningful, positive interactions.

And that's why schools suspend students. Few discipline options are left. Students can't be made to write sentences, or stand in the corner, or sit in the hall, or stay after school. Students can't even be made to wash desks when they're caught writing on them. No matter how grievous the infraction or how repetitive the offender, many parents refuse to allow school personnel to mete out punishment of any kind.

If a student is suspended for something seemingly trivial, such as disrupting class, most likely it was several days of disrupting class that resulted in that referral to the office. And often students are suspended for their *response* to a reprimand. For example, a student probably won't be suspended for turning around in his seat and talking during a lesson. But if you ask him to face front and pay attention and he responds with "Fuck off" he will be suspended for that.

Things like peer mediation, anger counseling, and restorative justice are fine and dandy, but if parents were doing their job, school districts would not have to spend time and money on the facility, staff and training necessary to implement those programs.

Let's put the blame back in its rightful place. It's the parents. It's always the parents. If you don't teach your child the meaning of the word "no," if you send your child to school believing that he does not have to follow rules, if he does not know how to share and play fair and be quiet when someone else is talking, then do not be surprised when you eventually get a call because your child has been suspended. You have not done your job to ensure that your child knows how to function in society.

It doesn't work both ways. Schools can't be required to raise academic standards and achievement and be expected to do it with troublemakers in the classroom.

As a country we need to decide: Are schools in the business of teaching and learning? Or are schools in the business of social work?

They don't have the resources to do both.

. . . OR NOT TO SUSPEND?

Suspending students from school is a crappy discipline tactic. Don't think for a minute that school personnel don't know it. They know it's illogical to suspend a kid for skipping. They know it's senseless to suspend a kid all day, when he misbehaved in one class. They know that kids purposely work the suspension system to get time off.

They know all of that. They're just hard-pressed for options. Alternatives cost money, and there's never enough of that.

It's important to note, though, that most public schools are not full of out-of-control students. Most classes on most days run smoothly. A lot of learning takes place.

But it would be irresponsible and inaccurate not to acknowledge that the number of, and severity of, discipline problems has increased, while punishment options have decreased.

The "Yeah? What you gonna' do about it?" kids are the worst. No matter how offensive their behavior, they know they can't be touched, embarrassed, humiliated or offended, so they challenge authority. Once they have that attitude, forget it. They might as well be suspended, because they'll be insufferable in class. It's a relief to see those kids go.

But for most infractions by basically good kids, suspension is a bad option. They get behind on their schoolwork, and worse, they have too much fun at home. An astounding number of parents do not reinforce a suspension punishment, and allow kids to sleep, watch television, and play video games all day. It's beyond aggravating when a kid returns from suspension bragging about the fun he had.

A good in-school suspension program or Saturday detention program is a place kids do *not* want to go. It is not fun. In a good program, if they don't bring schoolwork, plenty is provided for them. They're completely isolated from friends. No sleeping. No talking.

A bad in-school suspension program or Saturday detention program allows kids to sleep, play cards, eat, drink pop, talk, and hang out with friends. Even if they have to give up a Saturday, as punishment goes, it's still pretty fun.

The intention of such programs is punishment with no missed school. But any program is only as effective as the person in charge of it. And a good program is expensive. It requires a classroom, preferably off the beaten path—not easy to come by in crowded schools where every room is in use every hour. And it requires trained staff—preferably a teacher, to assign and help with schoolwork.

Ideally, every school would have an in-school suspension program for disruptive students.

And, in a perfect world, districts would have the power to make the parents sit right there next to them.

"IS TARDY THE SAME AS LATE?"

Were you late for work this week? Was your child late for school?

One of the most exasperating issues teachers deal with daily is student tardiness.

Most parents, though, have no idea just how disruptive tardiness is, not only to their child's education, but to the rest of the class, as well.

Picture this: The bell rings, kids are seated, teacher takes roll, logs it into the computer, and begins class. She's got their attention, the lesson is rolling along and five minutes later, bang! goes the door and in strolls Johnny. All heads turn to look, concentration broken. Teacher must stop the lesson, note the time, log back in and change Johnny's absence to a tardy, or the record will be inaccurate.

"So, what are we doing?" Johnny asks, and again teacher stops, this time to fill him in. Meanwhile, the rest of the class waits. If another student comes in late, they wait some more. Johnny has missed announcements, the introduction to the lesson, and the accompanying student questions. He starts class confused and behind.

For a parent or a student, the occasional tardy may seem inconsequential. But the cumulative effect for the teacher, who may have two or three tardy students each hour, is the stuff migraines are made of.

This is not just a high school problem. In fact, this disregard for punctuality starts at the elementary level and is taught and encouraged by parents. Elementary teachers often can't teach the first and last half hours of the day because so many parents drop off and pick up their kids at their own convenience.

These parents give lots of reasons for ignoring the school schedule: They want to beat the busses, they have other children to pick up or drop off, it suits *their* schedule, they overslept. But it's always disruptive because once the first parent arrives at the end of the day, the rest of the kids see it as the end of their school day, too, their minds turning to their own freedom.

The lack of respect for the school schedule trickles down to the child, resulting in disrespect for education in general, and a disregard for the sanctity of the classroom specifically.

The second part of the equation is the attitude that comes with the tardy. High school students think that if they're late for a "real" reason, like a flat tire, they're not really late. And they'll vehemently defend their lateness with, "It's not my fault!" followed by "I'm not responsible for this information—I wasn't here!"

Tardy policies always allow for a few real emergencies. But teens often think they can use those for dawdling at the drinking fountain, and tardies beyond their control should go unpunished. How do you teach them that tardy is tardy, when their parents have taught them it's not?

Parents hold the key to teaching the importance of punctuality.

When it comes to being late, if you're living it, they're learning it.

IT'S NOT A CORRESPONDENCE COURSE, YOU KNOW

Okay folks, we can't teach them if they aren't here.

Student attendance. It can make or break a child's education. And unfortunately, it absolutely consumes the time of teachers, principals, and secretaries, compromising the efficiency of the entire staff in the constant chase to play catch-up with absent kids.

It's important to note that the problem isn't absenteeism due to legitimate illness. School personnel are happy to work with parents and students there. And plenty of kids have good attendance.

But the attendance problem is getting worse, not better. To some, school is merely a correspondence course, where they drop in occasionally to pick up assignments.

Unfortunately, far too many parents work the scam, too. Instead of setting a good example and backing the attendance policy set by the school district, some parents join their kids in looking for every loophole.

But it's the trivial reasons kids miss school that drive teachers crazy.

Rebecca says she didn't come to school because the rain would mess up her hair. Andrea says she didn't come because she didn't have time to wash her hair. "I slept in" is a universal excuse, but one that kids believe to be perfectly legitimate. Some miss the bus and have no other way to get to school. Others are just too cool to ride the bus, and won't come if they can't get a ride. Many stay home to babysit younger siblings. Reggie's mom called in and said he was sick while he was sitting right in class. Reggie hadn't gone home the night before, and instead of worrying about that, Mom covered for him. Sam missed school to attend a party for his grandpa who was just released from prison.

The excuses are astonishing.

States have upped the ante on documentation. They require immaculate attendance records because attendance is tied to state funding. Gone are the days when teachers scrawled the names of absent students on a slip of paper and clipped it to the door. Attendance policies have become a fine art as schools strive for the right balance between accountability and fairness, in a policy that is clear and easy to follow, with minimal paperwork for all.

Because so many parents do try to work the system, the paperwork can be intense, requiring signatures in triplicate by student, parent, and teacher, complicated forms, and elaborate appeals processes.

But documentation is only half the problem. Providing students with material they missed is almost a full time job in itself. And truly, spending half an hour on makeup work for a student who stayed home to watch a wedding on *The Young and the Restless* exasperates even the most patient teacher.

And once again, it's the cumulative effect that takes its toll. If only one or two kids are absent a day, it's manageable. But often three to four students an hour miss class for no good reason. That adds up to fifteen to eighteen absent kids per day.

Most teachers are more than willing to go all out to help a kid with a legitimate excuse for being absent, cheerfully tutoring them at lunch or after school.

But think about it. If a student has missed an entire lecture, class discussion, or lab, how can he get caught up? The lesson can't be recreated after the fact and still maintain its integrity, with all its subtle nuances. And if they missed a quiz or a test, a makeup session has to be scheduled after school or at lunch, often with a different version of the test.

Kids need to be in school to succeed in school. Ask any teacher and they'll tell you that the reason most kids fail is because they have poor attendance. And unfortunately, attendance policies can make it seem like teachers spend more time on the kids they didn't teach than the ones they did.

The trend to hold truancy sweeps in neighborhoods and communities is a good start toward improving student attendance, but they make one tactical error.

They should pick up the parents, not the kids.

Round up the parents of the chronically truant kids, put them in a squad car and take them down to the station. Then make them sit through a parenting class. After all, that's where the problem starts, and until the parents are inconvenienced, the truancy problem will continue.

The kids who are not coming to school, who are being allowed to sleep in and then lie around and watch television all day, are the ones who probably most need to be in school, if for no other reason than to spend as little time as possible under the influence of parents who don't value education.

GRAB THAT TEACHABLE MOMENT

"Mom, look!" she squeals. "Look at this book! I love this book!"

She dances around in the aisle, dressed in pink from head to toe, blond curls bouncing.

"Remember, I read that one about the girl and the pig, and—"

Mom taps her foot and sighs with impatience. She doesn't look down at the little girl.

"Mom, remember? Remember the story my teacher read to us? The one about the horse? Mom, look, this book is like that one!"

Mom taps the CD she is about to purchase and stares straight ahead.

"Mom, we had a book fair at school and Jennifer won a prize and it was the book about the—"

Yank.

A hard jerk nearly pulls the little girl's arm out of the socket. "Be quiet! Stand still!" snaps the mother.

This parent/child exchange takes place in a bookstore. And as the sparkle and enthusiasm disappear from the little girl's eyes and her excitement fades away, the teacher in line behind them feels sick to her stomach, uncomfortable and sad and totally ticked off at the mom for dashing her daughter's spirits.

She wants to yank *her* by the arm and say, "Hey, do you have any idea what amazing worlds books can open up for your daughter? Do you know how well her enthusiasm for books will serve her through school, and on into the rest of her life? Do you know what a comfort a well-loved book can be? Do you know just how precious it is to have a child who loves books, especially now when the dazzling lights and sounds of technology have all but taken over? Do you? *Do you?*

"Look lady, you've got five, maybe ten minutes to wait in this line, and you're surrounded by books, something that obviously thrills this child. Use this teachable moment.

"Talk about books and stories and characters and adventure. Cultivate her love of books. Encourage her."

The teacher wants to swoop in and take the little girl by the hand and let her describe every single detail of every single book she ever read. She wants to show her all of the books she loved at her age, like *Little House in the Big Woods* and *The Boxcar Children.*

It's a feeling she can't shake for a long time.

A conversation about books wouldn't cost that mom a dime. But it would be an enormous investment in the future, just the same.

THE HONEYMOON IS OVER

The honeymoon is over.

Actually, honeymoons ain't what they used to be. The honeymoon for teachers is that first few weeks of school when the kids are on their very best behavior, when they wear their new school clothes, bring all of their bright and shiny school supplies, and answer politely when spoken to.

But the honeymoon seems to get shorter every year. Now it's more like a night at Motel 6 than two weeks at Club Med.

In some classes, there isn't a honeymoon at all. Ms. Quindlen's freshman English class burst into the room on the first day of school, started talking, and didn't stop.

Ever.

"Hey, what's going on with these freshmen?" exclaimed Kirstie, her senior student assistant. "Aren't they supposed to be nice for at least a few days? They act like this is the last day of school, not the first."

The honeymoon used to last much, much longer. A teacher could always count on at least a month of good behavior from their students. But years of having free rein at home has made many kids think that they have free rein at school, too.

For some, the honeymoon ends when interim reports go home. Most schools send interim reports of some kind halfway through the marking period. (Parents, it would be a good idea if you got to the mailbox first. And remind your child that tampering with the U.S. Mail is a federal offense.)

Some parents get a rude awakening when they realize that their child is not telling them what's really going on in class. The interim report sounds the alarm. It's not a recorded grade that goes on transcripts, but merely a communication to parents and students about how they're doing so far.

Often, the biggest surprise for parents is that their child isn't turning in assignments.

"I don't get it," they'll say to Johnny. "I bought $100 worth of school supplies last month and you haven't turned in sixteen assignments?"

In the next breath they'll turn to the teacher and say, "But I always ask Johnny if he has any homework, and he always says, 'No.'" (It's amazing that so many parents admit this.)

What's the polite way to say this?

Johnny is lying.

And the fact that he is lying is a personal problem, not the teacher's problem, so don't expect the teacher to solve it. (And aren't you embarrassed that you haven't made it your business to know?)

Parents shouldn't expect the teacher to call every time a child misses an assignment, either. Do the math; a parent has one (or two, or three) children. The teacher has as many as 150. A parent lives with the child. The child's teacher sees him for about fifty-five minutes a day, fifty-five minutes that are shared with approximately thirty other kids. A parent has known the child all of his life. The child's teacher barely knows him and won't know him well for a while.

By sending interim reports, schools are communicating grade information to parents every four to five weeks. That's eight times a year. In between, parents need to do their part. There's plenty of time to correct poor study habits and raise those grades before the first report card.

The honeymoon for teachers is much too short.

When that interim report gets home, it may be over for Johnny, too.

SPOILED ATHLETES ROT SCHOOL POLICIES

It's not a bit surprising that pro athletes think the world revolves around them. Why wouldn't they? It has since they first picked up a ball and ran with it.

No doubt about it, we live in a sports-crazy culture. Athletes get all kinds of special treatment. Favors are granted. They're bailed out of trouble. Bad behavior is excused. They are idolized beyond all reason. Their salaries and perks are exorbitant.

And it all starts in high school.

All kinds of allowances are made for high school athletes, every day. They are excused from school for athletic events, infractions of school rules are ignored, teachers are pressured, grades get changed.

It's wrong. It's unfair. And it's true.

One young star athlete arrived fifteen minutes late to his English class fourteen times in nine weeks. In the middle of the lesson he'd stroll in, carrying a pass from the principal. He'd take his time getting to his chair, look around the room, then look at the teacher and say, "So, what are we doing?" Office workers reported that he and the principal were simply sitting in the office talking sports every day.

Every school has an academic eligibility policy. Some are more strict than others. But the policy is only as strong as the people who enforce it. The easiest way around it is to pressure the classroom teacher into making allowances for the athlete. Most teachers have had coaches, parents, and even principals knock on their door in the middle of their lesson to find out what a particular athlete could do to pass. "C'mon," they'll ask, "can't he just do a report or something?"

When a kid isn't eligible to play his sport, some parents would rather blame anyone but their child. The child may have neglected to turn in ten assignments, and the parents will call it a "personality conflict" with the teacher. Sometimes they demand, and get, a class change to a different (i.e. easier) teacher past the deadline for class changes, though other students don't get that privilege. Sometimes parents resort to begging, using guilt about that child's future to pressure the teacher.

Some teachers won't give in, and choose to keep their standards high. Ironically, these teachers are often labeled "spoilsports" or considered not to be team players. Their school spirit is questioned. If they're female they're dubbed "old biddies."

If parents can't change the teacher, they might go after the eligibility policy itself.

At Mr. Wolfe's school, they had an efficient, computerized eligibility procedure in place. Each week teachers were given a list of athletes that were in their particular classes. With a minimum of fuss, a teacher could figure each athlete's cumulative GPA, and simply check off whether they were failing or near failing. It went straight to the coaches, fast and easy.

In Mr. Wolfe's American Literature class was an outstanding football player, Bobby Jensen, who was placed on the near-failing list several times. Just before a big game when college scouts would be in attendance he fell to the failing list. He claimed that he had no idea he was failing, even though his teachers had been following procedure.

His parents claimed he didn't know. They called central administration and voila! Suddenly a whole new step was added to the system. Now, in addition to telling students they were near failing, and sending the list to the coach, the teachers had to take the list around to each athlete and get their signature as well, to prove that they were told that they were on it.

Even though he was failing, Bobby got to play in that game. And the message that sent to the entire student body was, "If you're special, the rules will be rearranged for you." Not surprisingly, this angered the "ordinary" kids. They knew they would not likely receive such favoritism.

There's a lot to be learned from school sports: good sportsmanship, teamwork, self-discipline. And no doubt athletics have kept many a kid out of trouble. But why do we feel compelled to bend all the rules for gifted athletes? Why do we put them on a pedestal? After all, it's not as if the world couldn't get along without sports.

Maybe it's unrealistic to expect a school not to reflect society's love of sports and athletes.

But must we be accomplices in creating athletes without character?

UP CLOSE AND PERSONAL

She was sixteen years old, driving down Leroy Street in her hometown of Fenton, Michigan, when she passed Ms. Shapiro, her English teacher, driving the other way.

She nearly drove off the road.

She had never seen a teacher outside of school. She didn't know what she thought—she knew teachers didn't live at school. But she didn't imagine that they drove around in little blue Ford Pintos, either.

The age of discovery is different for everyone, but it's a nearly universal experience to learn—with surprise—that your teacher is human.

Some teachers go to great lengths to hide their humanity, believing that mystery breeds respect. They present themselves as teacher, and nothing but.

Others give students a highly orchestrated peek into their lives, building a persona around past football prowess or the fact that they drive a Harley. They know that if they plant the seed, the legend will grow. And some go out of their way to be as accessible as possible, because you just never know what might build a bridge to a student. They share their lives freely, telling stories about their children, pets, hobbies, and vacations, always looking for a connection.

Sometimes, oddly enough, that personal stuff is the only memory a child takes from a class. Linda remembers nothing about first grade, except the time her teacher, Ms. Remington, brought her fancy new party dress to class on a hanger, and told the class all about her impending dinner date with a new man. They were fascinated. Linda remembers the exact look on her mom's face, too, when she relayed the story to her that afternoon.

A close encounter outside of school can be unsettling to student and teacher alike. Ms. Berg will never forget the time she ran into one of her students on a beach in upper Michigan. She was young, her bikini was small, and that poor seventh grader nearly got eyeball whiplash trying to look anywhere but at her.

Another time Ms. Berg came out of a bathroom stall in a local nightclub, and found one of her tenth graders primping at the mirror. It's hard to say whose gasp was louder. "Oh my God, please, don't tell my mom!" the girl cried, agog at the sight of her teacher standing in a nightclub bathroom.

It's a fine line teachers walk. They know that if their students see another side of them, separate from the one that nags them to put their names on their paper, it can for some reason be the spark that makes students like them, which in turn makes them remember to put their names on their paper.

That's the thing about education; when you get right down to it, it's more about people—good, bad, silly, indifferent, flawed, funny, ordinary people—than anything else.

HOVERCRAFTS, TAKE OFF

Oh, it's a love/hate relationship teachers have with their students' parents, no doubt about it.

But with problem parents, the verdict is out on which parent is worse; the absent parent that can't be reached by phone and never comes to conferences, or the "hovercrafts," that new breed of parent that is umbilically, weirdly, voraciously, obsessively, neurotically overinvolved with their kids.

It's become such an issue that some schools have added rules to their handbooks, stipulating the appropriate extent of parental involvement. Websites are devoted to teaching parents how to let go. Some colleges are even addressing the issue at freshman orientation.

Sasha's mom demanded (not asked) that the teacher send her a signed note describing the day's' assignment, whether Sasha did it, the quality of the work, and her classroom behavior. Every single day. Imagine, for a moment, if the parent of every child made such a request. The girl was a freshman who earned mostly Bs and Cs.

The teacher complied because, believe it or not, it was easier than arguing with her. She knew this mom would never see it from her harried perspective. She knew this parent would never understand that she was cheating her daughter out of an important learning experience. There were several other processes already in place for students to keep track of their own assignments, processes designed to teach them personal responsibility.

That's the thing about overinvolved parents. They are unwilling to let their child assume responsibility for their own actions. They want to orchestrate their child's world completely, and in the public school system, they usually can. But what happens when that child goes out into a world that doesn't dance to Mom and Dad's tune?

Hovercraft parents also believe that they are the only ones who have their child's best interests at heart. That's not true, of course, but it often puts them at odds with the other adults in the child's life.

What's more, they can't imagine that a teacher could know anything about their child that they don't know. But teachers do. They see a child in a completely different context. That can reveal some very cool things about a kid. And some not so cool, which hovercraft parents do not believe anyway.

No one is advocating parental neglect. Goodness knows there's too much of that. And teachers do want open communication with parents.

The problem with hovercrafts is that they're hovering so close they lose sight of the big picture. They can't see that the most essential lesson a parent will ever teach a child is to be self-sufficient.

WORK IT, BABY

If you're not getting everything you want from the public school system, you're just not trying.

Because there's no doubt that some parents are. Some parents work the system like pros. They get the teachers they want, they get the classes they want, and all too often they get the discipline they want. Some even get the curriculum changed the way they want it.

Don't misunderstand. Parental involvement is not a bad thing. It's a good thing. But it's interesting to note how really clever, even downright diabolical, some parents are at getting what they want, while other parents remain clueless about the power they hold.

Ms. Gilbert was exhausted by the attendance policy at her school. Every time a student missed her class she had to fill out a form, sign it, have the student sign it, file a copy, give the student a copy, and send a copy to the attendance office. A five-inch ring binder sat on the corner of her desk, holding hundreds of signed and alphabetized forms, organized by hour.

In spite of being told that more than nine absences not made up would result in failure, seniors didn't take it seriously. The notebook bulged.

At the end of the year, when parents clued in that their children were not going to graduate, they started working the system. It was painful to watch. The majority of parents managed to get their kids off so they could graduate, while those with less savvy parents didn't get to walk on graduation night. It was flat out unfair all the way around.

It was a rotten message to send to the absent students, too; attendance is not important, and parents will bail you out of trouble. But it was terribly distressing to watch only a few take the punishment that all deserved.

And that's the rub when parents figure out ways around the rules. There's nothing wrong with looking out for a child's interests. Yet it's so unfair to the ones who don't have parents who advocate for them.

Should school districts be receptive to their clientele? Absolutely. In fact, smart school officials work with this parental phenomenon, instead of against it. They cultivate parental involvement, and channel it where they need it most. Smart school officials know that everyone is more cooperative if they feel some ownership in the proceedings.

Smart school officials also communicate clearly and often with parents, because nothing makes a parent more ornery than feeling like information is being withheld.

School officials walk a fine line. They must hold a vision of the big picture, but still appease individuals. They need to recognize self-serving parental intentions and respond to them in the context of what's best for all.

Parents walk a fine line, too. Look out for your kid, but pay attention to the lesson your advocacy teaches.

Every school system, public or private, has parents who work the system and get unfair advantages. And it's not just schools, of course. In society, rules are finessed every day.

The squeaky wheel really does get the grease. So if you're not a power player in your child's public school experience, get crackin'.

Just make sure to use your powers for good.

And not evil.

INFLATION TARNISHES THOSE SHINY A's

There's a dirty little secret that school administrators don't want you to know. Grade inflation is alive and well, even in your school.

Education has gone the way of dentists and ambulance chasers, and schools are practically advertising on street corners to lure clients. It's a competitive business and some schools play the game better than others, using slick videos and colorful brochures to tout the finer qualities of their school. And in the eyes of John and Jane Q. Public, a school where most of the students get good grades must be a better school.

Often a student's grade point average does not correlate with his ACT or SAT scores, which begs the question: Do the A students experience a brain melt the day of the test and do poorly?

No. It's called grade inflation and it's basically the slow erosion of educational requirements and standards. It's giving a student an A for B work, or passing a student with a D- when he has actually failed. It's a teacher requiring less for an A than they did five years ago.

Administrators don't come right out and tell teachers to lower standards to raise grades. But they don't tell them to raise standards, either. Administrators tell teachers to improve student learning.

Well, duh. Teachers would dance the cha-cha or eat flies if they thought it would help their students learn. That's why teachers use their own time and their own money to attend conferences, workshops, seminars, and classes, looking for that magic elixir that will ignite a spark of interest in the video-game-glazed eyes of their students.

Most teachers would rather clean the school cafeteria on fish stick Friday than give a student a grade he doesn't deserve. But the pressure from administrators and parents takes its toll.

When students get to high school where the work is decidedly more difficult, and grade point averages count for college admission, suddenly an A student may struggle to get a B. The stunned parent pressures the teacher by telling the principal (and anyone else who will listen) that Johnny isn't a B student, he's never gotten Bs, and the offending teacher must not be very good if he can't see that Johnny is an A student.

It's as if the sheer force of their will can make it so. And often it does.

There are countless ways that teachers are pressured to inflate grades. When Mr. Baldacci complained to the assistant principal that his students weren't doing their homework, the principal replied, "Then maybe you shouldn't give homework."

Most administrators are more subtle, though. The message may come through an administrator who pleads the case of an ineligible athlete before a big game. The message may come through an administrator who calls a teacher into his office to have a little chat about the number of students who have earned Es in his class.

There are other subtle ways to manipulate grade point averages. Some districts have adopted a district-wide grade policy that states a student must be given 40 percent on any assignment in any class, *even if they did not complete the assignment.* Others have adopted policies that allow students to retake course tests as many times as they want, all semester, until they get the grade they want.

Teachers are not blameless when it comes to grade inflation. Nobody likes to see hard work go unrewarded, especially in an environment where laziness abounds, so sometimes teachers raise a student's grade a bit for extra effort. And kids and administrators alike know which teachers in a school are the "easy" teachers and which ones are "hard."

Now that the push nationwide is to tie teacher evaluations to student performance, the problem will only get worse.

The bottom line is this: Now that schools are competing for clients, fair and accurate student assessment often falls victim to the money game.

Your student's A may not be the same A you earned in high school.

TOO MUCH STUFF

Before birthdays and holidays, many teenagers hand their parents a list. But before going hog wild at the mall, take a moment and think about what a child really needs.

It's easy to buy a bunch of stuff that's going to break or go out of style. It is much more difficult to teach the value of a dollar and the meaning of hard work.

Of course there's nothing wrong with having nice things. It's the *attitude* about the things that can be a problem. Teachers tend to look for the lesson in everything. And the lesson they see being sent to many kids is that everything will be handed to you, everything is disposable, and if you lose it, don't worry, we'll get you another one.

The message, of course, that teachers want to see given to students is that you get what you earn and if you lose it, there will be consequences.

The halls and classrooms of a high school tell the story.

For example, in a high school, small change is, well, small change. Kids can't be bothered to pick it up. When Mr. Wolfe stopped to pick up a nickel off the floor in the hall, Jessica, a student in his senior English class, acted as if he was picking a sandwich out of the garbage.

"Mr. Wolfe!" she whispered. "I can't believe you picked that up! I'm *sure*, how *embarrassing!"*

Mr. Wolfe grinned and jingled the coins in his pocket. On the way out of the building he picked up enough change to buy a king-size Snickers at the Quik-Stop on his way home.

Pens and pencils are, in the minds of kids, disposable, too. At the end of the day the floor is littered with them. Never mind that half the students never have a pen or pencil when they need it. Hundreds of them still end up on the floor.

And textbooks? Well, as far as many kids are concerned, those five-pound, sixty dollar books are disposable, too. They're carelessly left everywhere: the classroom, the hall, the cafeteria, the bus—and even occasionally the side of the road after being tossed out the window of the bus.

And what's even more astounding is that at the end of the year, when kids are offered the opportunity to go through the huge pile of unclaimed books on the chance that their book was turned in by someone else, they won't do it. Most won't take the time to look through the pile, but would rather let their parents pay the sixty dollars to replace it. It might take a student perhaps half an hour to go through the pile. Would you work for $120 an hour?

The lost and found in a high school tells a story, too. You could clothe a small village with what is sitting in the lost and found. Dozens of pairs of eyeglasses. Jeans. Hoodies. Expensive jackets. Jewelry. Cameras. Hundred dollar tennis shoes. Full book bags. Notebooks. A suit coat left after the homecoming dance. Even photo albums.

Pennies, pencils and textbooks may seem trivial, but the lessons must start somewhere.

Don't buy into society's notion that if a kid doesn't have everything that every other kid has, he's going to be scarred for life. Stuff breaks and goes out of style.

But the lessons learned about the *value* of that stuff, those will last a lifetime.

PROM PAPARAZZI

It was spring of 1976. Her mom snapped one last picture as she and her date pulled away from the curb in his mother's wood paneled Vista Cruiser station wagon. And happily, that was the last they saw of their parents on prom night. Back then, prom was a chance to dress up, go off into the night alone, and act like a grown-up. At the dance, real grown-ups—the teachers—watched unobtrusively from the shadows and talked quietly among themselves, stifling yawns.

Mercy, how things have changed.

High school proms have reached epic proportions, as kids try to out-do each other on a small-time version of the Hollywood red carpet. But on a night that is supposed to be a teen's debut into the world of adults, many parents can't seem to strike the right balance between hovering and looking the other way.

Instead of waving good-bye at the door, many parents literally follow their kids to the prom. Because the arrival is everything, folks line both sides of the entrance, a parental paparazzi lying in wait. Bedazzled kids step from limos into flashing strobes and whirring camcorders as parents strain to capture every precious second of the long red carpet walk.

You'd think parents would pack up and go home then, but they don't. The parental unit, sometimes dragging along younger brothers and sisters, follows the kids into the prom, recording their every move from the buffet line to the prom picture line. Like some bizarre reality show, nothing is too trivial to capture on film.

Ironically, and perhaps by tacit agreement with their children, they often leave just when they should stay, and miss what they need to see; teachers repeatedly reminding students that their dancing is too dirty, and if they don't stop they'll have to leave. Those parental shutterbugs don't venture to the after-prom festivities in the rented hotel room, either. What Kodak moments are they missing there?

The look-at-me generation seems to equate a good time with the size of the spectacle. But it's a school dance, not a coronation. For the kid's part, how can prom possibly live up to the hype and expense that currently surround it? Do they actually have any fun? Do they know how to have fun without being the center of attention? Isn't all that pressure terribly stressful?

If you think your only job as a parent is to be your child's biggest fan, then you've taught a fine lesson in narcissism and entitlement.

But how on earth will your child cope when the rest of the world doesn't find him quite so fascinating?

SENIORS, TAKE HEED

It's most unbecoming to beg.

So seniors, heed this: if you let the senioritis bug bite you, you may spend your last days of school begging.

Begging your teachers to pass you, that is.

It happens every year and it is a pitiful sight every time. At least one student completely blows off the last marking period of his senior year, ignores all warnings from teachers, fails a class, loses a credit, and ends up not graduating. So that last day of school, which should be filled with nostalgia and celebration, instead becomes a sorrowful experience as he begs his teacher to please, please, please, pass him so he can walk on graduation day.

Sometimes it works. Sometimes it doesn't. Either way, it is wrenching for all involved. And whatever students may think of their teachers, when students fail it is as painful for the teacher as it is for the student.

So seniors take heed. Once you return from spring break (and whatever temptations you faced there) the temptation to let it all go and revel in your senior status will be as alluring as the smell of a flame-broiled Whopper.

True, the sprint to the finish line is stressful. Significant life decisions about college or jobs can fill even the most level-headed student with self-doubt. Stress is one reason seniors give in; it's easier to decree that senioritis has claimed mind and body than to make the hard decisions.

Ironically, right when students need to be in top form to pull it all together, they are hit with a lassitude that, real or not, can be contagious. "I have senioritis!" becomes synonymous with "I don't want to do any work today," and can start a dangerous chain reaction. To teens it's an accepted rite of passage, one that feels wickedly fun, to boot.

Demands for end-of-year projects at school compete with distractions at home where there's often a frenzy of home-improvement projects in preparation for the graduation open house. And it's expensive to be a senior. Senior pictures, graduation announcements, new clothes, prom, and open houses all take their toll on the family budget.

This is not the time for parents to relax their own vigilance. Parents should not take the role of enabler and ease up on the rules. Consistency is key. Don't be afraid to be the heavy.

And remember, academics are not the only way a senior year can go awry. A prank that seems harmless can have devastating disciplinary consequences, too.

So seniors, please, don't make your teachers deliver that one final lesson; you are accountable for the work and will fail if you don't do it.

Finish what you started. You can choose for this to be a joyful, productive time, or you can choose to disappoint your parents, and ultimately, yourself.

Choose wisely.

Chapter Four

Community

From school safety and shuffled children to life in the fishbowl and dancing on cars

Never doubt that a small group of thoughtful, concerned citizens can change the world. Indeed it is the only thing that ever has.

—Margaret Mead

THE BUILDING SPEAKS . . .

My name is John F. Kennedy High School. I am a public school, an institution of learning, paid for and owned by the people in my community. I was built in 1965 in a suburb of an industrial, blue-collar city.

Thousands of students have passed through my halls. Some have gone on to do great things, to become doctors and artists and humanitarians. Some, I'm sad to say, have not done well. A few have landed in prison.

To many, I am just a building, cold brick and steel, drab institutional colors adorning my walls. But I am more than just a building. I am the heart of the community, opening my doors to one and all. When school is not in session, college and enrichment classes, elections, even craft fairs are held here. I don't discriminate on religion, color, or creed, though sometimes the people inside of me do.

I've seen many changes since my doors opened in 1965. I watched as typewriters were carried out and computers were brought in. I saw 8 mm projectors replaced by TVs, then VCRs, and then DVD players. I saw slide rules replaced by calculators.

My biggest challenge now (and also for my people) is to keep up with technology. My wiring is old and not equipped to take the strain of hundreds of computers, printers, scanners, televisions, and fax machines. Gang plugs and outlet strips have been added everywhere, but still, sometimes it's just too much and I blow a fuse.

In the 1970s my glass windows were replaced with energy efficient panels, making my classrooms and hallways dark. In the 1980s my terrazzo floors were covered with carpet in an effort to soundproof my rooms. In the 1990s the carpet was taken back out because some of my students had allergies to mold and dust trapped in that carpet.

My large, spacious classrooms have been divided into smaller classrooms to accommodate special education classes. My metal shop was replaced with a modern technology lab. My charming old-fashioned chalkboards have been replaced with white dry-erase boards and smelly erasable markers.

My cafeteria has gone from serving real meals on real plates with real utensils, to serving fast food on Styrofoam plates with plastic utensils. No one makes kids clean up after themselves anymore, however, and after lunch my floors are littered with candy wrappers and food, my tables covered with abandoned milk cartons and water bottles. Amid much controversy, pop machines were installed in the 1980s only to be taken back out twenty years later.

For the most part, I am well cared for. My custodians sweep my floors and tend to my ailments, but my students seem to be increasingly careless. They stuff paper towels into my toilets for the pleasure of watching them run over, and empty my soap dispensers onto the floor. Gum and graffiti are everywhere.

So many fads have come and gone. Long, unwashed hippie hair, afros, mall bangs, mullets. Saggy pants, tattoos, piercings, goth. My floors have been traversed by everything from canvas Converse sneakers, to ridiculously expensive leather Nikes. Platform shoes and bellbottoms went out of style and came back again. I even remember when female teachers were not allowed to wear slacks.

I have felt the trepidation of the freshmen's first day and the exuberance of the seniors' last. Love, hate, anger, jealousy, joy, grief, sorrow. I am witness to all of the drama that unfolds here day after day, as children make the transition from adolescence to adulthood.

The students, the support staff, the principals, the teachers. I love and embrace them all.

If my walls could talk, oh, the stories they would tell. . .

... About the Kids

Thousands of students have come through my doors since I opened in 1965, and though their clothing and hairstyles have changed, their hopes and fears have not.

Omniscience has granted me the power to see into the hearts and minds of all who walk my halls. If only they could see each other as clearly as I see them.

Rick is one of my more troubled students. He has endured many labels during his time in the public school system. Slow learner. Misfit. Loner. Degenerate.

Rick's stepfather smacked his mother, hard, right across the mouth before he left for school this morning. Rick hates his stepfather, with a hatred so deep it makes his gut ache. He wanted to step in, to beat the crap out of the pig, but his mother, blood oozing from the corner of her mouth, just screamed at him to get out, to go to school.

He hates school. He hates home, too. But there was nothing he could do if he stayed. The creep and his mother were still half crocked from the night before, and would pass out soon anyway, only to wake up in time to drink their dinner again.

He's angry with his mother for staying with the creep, ashamed to come from where he does. He's angry, too, at his real dad for leaving when Rick was only three. His face is dark with anger as he steps off the bus, roughly pushing a puny freshman out of the way. He ducks into the bathroom and lights up, then takes out his pocketknife and carves a deep gash into the freshly painted stall door, picturing the creep's face.

Tessa has her own problems. Bookish and brilliant, she has wanted to be a surgeon since her parents told her so when she was six years old. She gets off the bus and heads straight for the library, eager to do some research before the first bell.

The other kids call her Teacher's Pet, and the teachers do love her, simply because she makes their job so easy. For her, learning is effortless, but the other kids make her pay for this. She, too, has endured many labels, given to her by other students. Nerd. Braniac. Four-eyes. Einstein. The name-calling hurts, but she pretends that it doesn't.

Tessa is stressed. Her parents are both surgeons and they expect her to be making the Dean's List at Harvard in exactly two years. When she thinks about the possibility of not getting in her stomach cramps and her heart races.

Other students are simply lost in the crowd. Like Brooke, who feels insignificant. An outsider. Timid and wary, she shuffles through the halls with her head down. She is an average looking girl who gets average grades. She doesn't cause trouble and she is often overlooked or ignored. Her sixth hour teacher still doesn't know her name.

Brooke is rarely absent, never tardy, and has never been sent to the office. She doesn't play sports, is not in any clubs, and doesn't have any close friends. Boys look right through her and she knows it. No one has bothered to label her anything.

If only my students and teachers could know each other as well as I know them. They would be kinder to each other, the rites of adolescence would be easier, and high school wouldn't seem like such a mean, cold place.

. . . About the Staff

The unsung heroes here are the support staff. And they are aptly named. They support, in dozens of ways, the teaching and learning that happens here.

Custodians, secretaries, cooks, bus drivers, teacher assistants. I could not function without them.

But the role of my custodians is misunderstood. My students think that my custodians are here for the sole purpose of cleaning up after *them*, when in fact they are here to look after *me*, to repair my windows, change my light bulbs and wax my floors. My custodians are not here to clean up after overindulged children.

It's regrettable. Their job is unnecessarily nauseating. It's true that in addition to building maintenance, they must clean up vomit and blood spills and unclog toilets.

But the sheer piggishness of kids can be stupefying. Are there no manners anymore? No sense of decorum at all? I wonder, sometimes, what their homes look like. Surely they are required to pick up after themselves there. Do high school kids play in their food at home? Do they walk through the living room dropping candy wrappers as they go?

I can feel Harry Schmidt's frustration. He shakes his head and sighs as he enters the cafeteria. Tray after tray left on the tables, in spite of the huge trash bins standing everywhere. For kicks, many kids pour the remains of their pop or milk into their leftover food, stirring it into a thick, smelly, goo. The trays are almost overflowing and Harry has to pick them up carefully, lest the flimsy Styrofoam bends and the goo spills all over the floor.

Is it a game to see who can make the biggest mess?

Ugh. It's enough to make him vomit. Some wise guy has stuffed a yellow condom full of peaches and stood it on end on the tray, then squeezed ketchup around it. Harry dumps it into the trashcan and moves on, wishing for hidden surveillance cameras. Their parents should see this.

There's probably enough wasted food here to feed at least one hundred hungry kids every day. Harry wonders why they buy the food if they don't want it. Even the brown bag lunches, lovingly packed by someone at home, are largely wasted, smashed and mutilated.

After school Harry sweeps the halls and classrooms in his wing. By the end of his route he has picked up twenty-three pens and pencils, twelve textbooks, six notebooks, and $2.36 worth of change.

A quiet, gentle soul, Harry is a church-going man, but he has ceased to be shocked at the filthy graffiti written on the desks. He has scrubbed the desks so many times in the sixteen years he's worked here that the finish is worn off.

He moves on to the most dreaded job of the day. The student bathrooms. He goes into the boys', hoping there's nothing too awful today.

Whew. It's not too bad. He flushes all of the toilets and urinals, wondering, again, if kids behave this way at home. Did no one teach them to flush a toilet after they use it? Using three different buckets and bleach, he cleans the toilets, sinks and floor, then shuffles out.

When parents send their children off to school, they place their trust in many: the bus drivers, who get them here safely, the secretaries, who handle their paperwork, the cooks who feed them.

And the custodians. Always in the background, but always there, taking care of me.

And everyone else.

. . . About the Administrators

Of all of the public servants that walk my halls, perhaps the role of building principal has changed the most since I opened my doors in 1965.

Then, most principals across the state were middle-aged white men. The principal of an elementary school was often the only man in a building full of female teachers. Now, fortunately, there is more diversity.

A good principal is a gift, a visionary offering guidance to students and teachers alike. A bad principal is a drain on the morale and energy of everyone, an inconsistent disciplinarian, allowing students and teachers to falter alone, without support or guidance.

In my early days, teachers worked their way up through the ranks to become principals in the district that they knew and loved. Now, principals are sought from other districts. Sometimes they bring with them a fresh approach and new ideas. But sometimes, in their zest to share those new ideas, they destroy the culture of a district they don't know and don't understand.

The very first principal to lead my teaching and learning family was Mr. Maxheimer, an affable and well-liked varsity football coach and P.E. teacher with a master's degree in administration. Early on, central administration made it clear to him that a principal's job was his whenever he was ready. Membership in the Good Ol' Boys Club sealed the deal and ensured his success.

In those days, being a principal was a pretty nice job. His secretaries and teachers worked hard and made him look good. Sure, sometimes he put in long hours, but there was always time to kick back and talk sports with the coaches. By and large, parents and students alike respected him, and when he made tough, unpopular decisions, he was commended for his leadership.

Ms. O'Connell is the current principal of my building, but she had to work twice as hard as Maxheimer did to get here. There's no time for leisure in her day. She arrives early, stays late, and eats lunch at her desk. Because she's a woman, she is scrutinized more closely. When she makes tough, unpopular decisions, she's called a bitch.

School districts have not escaped the insanity of our litigious society. Looking back, Mr. Maxheimer can only remember being threatened with a lawsuit twice in his career. Ms. O'Connell is threatened with lawsuits almost daily.

Both principals wish they could spend less time disciplining kids. But even discipline has changed since the 1960s. Kids used to beg the principal not to call their parents when they were in trouble, hoping to be spared more trouble when they got home.

Now even kids in serious trouble strut into the office, discipline referral in hand, and demand, "Get my mom on the phone. She'll be up here in ten minutes with our lawyer!"

Since Columbine, the responsibility of keeping her students safe weighs heavily on Ms. O'Connell. Safety issues take an increasing amount of her time, time that was already in short supply.

I feel for the leaders of my teaching and learning family. The leadership of a public school requires someone who understands the teaching and learning process. Unfortunately, more and more principals have backgrounds in business, but no experience in education whatsoever.

A principal's job used to be something to aspire to, a position of respect. But no more. Now it's a thankless job, one fewer and fewer people are willing to take.

... About the Teachers

I watch teachers trudge in and out of my building day after day, arms laden with papers and books. Omniscience has granted me the power to see into their hearts and minds, to see their concern for their students, their frustration, their exhaustion, their hope.

Ms. Daly is in her second year of teaching. She has wanted to teach her whole life, and she believes that she can make a difference. Deeply spiritual, her first year was quite an eye-opener. The coarse language and disrespect from her students shocks and offends her. The shy, quiet kids are drawn to her gentle demeanor, sensing a safe place, but the tough kids sense fear and, like animals, are quick to take advantage. She almost quit at the end of that first year, and still isn't sure she'll stay. But this is her dream, and she's not ready to let it go. The reality of the job is just so very different from what she imagined.

Mr. Wilde went to college to avoid the draft in 1966. Star of his high school football team, he chose to teach so that he could coach. The jocks like him because with a little prodding he'll stray from the lesson and tell game stories all hour. Turns out, he's not all that crazy about teaching, but as his seniority grew it didn't seem prudent to leave. Now, he's lost his courage. What else could he do, anyway? He's got three kids in college and can't entertain the idea of starting over. So he tells himself that he loves his job, tells himself that he is good at it.

The youngest on the staff, Ms. Campbell, is a top-notch teacher, engaging and enthusiastic. The kids like her because she's quick with a comeback, and doesn't take crap from any of them. But she feels that the sacrifices she makes to be here are just too great. Her friends, all bright and vibrant twenty-somethings, are already making more money than she does, with a limitless potential for more. Their jobs have perks, too, bonuses and freebies and trips and panache. She works long, hard hours and doesn't have the time, energy, or money her friends have. It's sad. She won't stay long. The world is her oyster and as much as she likes the kids, there's just not enough incentive for her to stay.

Every school has many good, competent teachers. Most have only a sprinkling of exceptional teachers. Ms. Garcia is exceptional. Mastery of subject, creativity, superior organizational skills, energy to burn, charm and charisma give her that certain something that even the most hardened kid can't resist. Just a little bit irreverent, she gets their attention and holds it. It helps that she doesn't have her own children and is able to spend all of her free time on schoolwork. Her lessons are so entertaining that kids leave her class amazed at how much they learned, amazed at how effortless it was.

You don't see what I see. Teachers here late at night, decorating their classrooms, working on lesson plans, grading papers. Tears privately shed over the sheer meanness of teenagers. Sore feet, aching backs, tired voices.

Our society has it all wrong; we pay professional athletes millions to play a game, and our teachers a pittance for educating our future.

And still they teach.

Every day.

DILIGENCE GETS KIDS THROUGH

"I just don't *understand*. She's always done so *well* in school."

That's the plaintive cry of the puzzled parents of freshmen after report cards come out. It's called the Freshman Phenomenon: Students who had been reasonably successful in K–8 suddenly, inexplicably, start doing poorly in school.

Ask any teacher and they will tell you that most students do not do poorly in school because they can't do the work. They do poorly in school because they won't do the work.

But the Freshman Phenomenon has more to do with growing pains than academics. During adolescence, students' brains are not yet mature in bodies that often are. There is a heightened interest in peer groups, and a great deal of social and emotional growth takes place. Different parts of the brain mature at different rates, causing moodiness and impulsivity, which explains why eighth graders always seem to operate at one of three speeds: uncontrollable giggling, yelling, or crying.

And since freshmen just got done being eighth graders, it's not surprising that they're still growing emotionally and socially.

At the root of the problem is a preoccupation with looks, popularity, social status, fitting in, and tantalizing distractions provided by older, streetwise kids. Freshmen girls, for example, fuss endlessly with their hair and makeup. By the time they're seniors, they stop. If you were to hear a tape of what goes through a freshman's mind, 98 percent of it would involve insecurity.

Preoccupation begets forgetfulness.

"But I saw you do that assignment!" parents exclaim. "Why didn't you turn it in?!"

"I forgot," the child shrugs, unconcerned.

Kids go from the relative safety of junior high, replete with warm fuzzies, to the fast, sometimes impersonal, pace of high school. As if getting around a large building isn't challenging enough, now their classes count for credit.

The work is more difficult and demanding and there's a lot less handholding. A late assignment is marked down, and missed assignments pile up fast. It's easy to fall so far behind they're too overwhelmed to catch up.

Work ethic is at issue, too. If a student hasn't been taught responsibility at home, they don't have the skills to buckle down when the going gets tough.

Another huge problem for freshmen is organization. Look into a freshman's book bag and you're likely to find a pile of crumpled paper. It's hard to know which comes first, the disorganized book bag or the disorganized mind, but either way it equals lost handouts and homework. For many freshmen, simply remembering to bring a textbook to class is a colossal feat.

The heartening news is that in most cases, freshmen pull it together by sophomore year. That's not good enough, though, because failed freshman classes put them behind in credits, compromising graduation.

We don't need more testing or a different curriculum to save our freshmen.

But we do need all hands on deck to guide them through this turbulent time.

PEOPLE LIKE THIS

When it comes to teenagers, adults are so concerned with putting out the big fires like drugs, alcohol abuse, violence, crime, and sex that they sometimes neglect the small things that make up the fabric of a polite society.

Many offenses that once would have been call-home-worthy now fall by the wayside. For example, it's not unusual to hear the "F" word shouted in the halls of a high school. Every day.

Really. Ask a high school teacher. They'll tell you, because they're shocked, too. They used to send kids to the principal's office for swearing but now, in light of all the really serious issues that administrators deal with, they often just tell students to watch their language.

Schools are simply a microcosm of society, so kids' behavior simply reflects what is going on elsewhere in the culture. For this generation, TV has been not only the babysitter, but also the role model. One look at the television line-up on any given night proves that society is pushing the boundaries of common sense and good taste all the time. Shows like *Jersey Shore* and MTVs *Spring Break* applaud bad manners and bad behavior.

Ms. Smith, a well-liked physics teacher known for playing practical jokes on her students, witnessed a perfect example of the decline of polite society while monitoring the hall between classes.

The girl involved is a sweet freshman named Josie. Pretty and fresh-faced, endearingly tall and gawky, Josie has a habit of ducking her head and looking shyly up from underneath her lashes. Her boyfriend is a year older, cocky and sure of himself, armed with a smart-alecky grin and the devil in his eye. Whenever they're together Josie is all atwitter and giddy, as if she just can't believe her good fortune at having such a catch for a boyfriend.

Ms. Smith is leaning against the wall in the hall watching the students go by, thinking about the tall stack of tests she has to grade tonight. She sees Josie and her bad boy come down the hall with their arms wrapped around each other's waists, pressed against each other all up and down the sides of their bodies. They're turned in at the hip, looking at each other. Josie is staring dreamily into his eyes, and he is grinning his smart-alecky grin back.

So cute. Josie is self-conscious but proud, hoping that everyone is looking at them and terrified that they might be.

The bell is about to ring so they must say their good-byes quickly and get to class.

Their faces move closer together.

Oh, great, Ms. Smith sighs to herself. *Big kissing scene. Now I'm going to have to bust them for a Public Display of Affection.*

Closer, closer, closer. . .

Just as Ms. Smith is about to move in, the boy, whose face is now about one inch from Josie's, lets out an enormous, loud, wet, disgusting burp.

Right into Josie's mouth.

Gasp!

Ms. Smith is so horrified she can hardly speak. Her eyes bug out of her head. She is absolutely riveted by this unbelievable turn of events.

Josie sees Ms. Smith watching and laughs, and tosses her head, and hugs the twerp as if to say, "It's okay, I don't mind, isn't he funny, isn't he wonderful?!"

The boy laughs out loud, smiling his smart-alecky grin. There's no question he did it on purpose.

It's a gross story. And sort of shocking. And that's the point. High school teachers witness a lot of things that the people they know would never do.

But they do know these people. And so do you. These are our people. This is our society.

So why don't these kids know better? Where did they get the idea that this was acceptable behavior? Why doesn't that boy know the proper way to treat a girl? And why doesn't Josie value herself enough to know that this is not okay?

We can't sit back and mutter under our breath, "What's wrong with kids today?"

Turn on your TV. Look at what is accepted and condoned.

The society we have created is what's wrong with kids today.

RUNAWAY LESSONS

Earnest, sweet, and oh-so-squirrelly.

That's what she forgot about junior high students.

When asked to speak to an eighth grade class about career choices, Ms. McCullough eagerly accepted. She has long maintained that this is an area where the public school system falls short. Far too little time is spent teaching kids about careers.

And having made a pretty significant mid-life career change herself, from teacher to writer, she felt she had some wisdom to share.

After ten years, it felt good to be back in the classroom, talking extemporaneously, moving up and down the aisles, bantering with thirteen-year-olds, drawing them out, focusing the wanderers. She was tickled to find that she still "had it."

Just like riding a bike, she thought. *You never forget this stuff.*

Her intention was to share with the students what no one shared with her as a youngster; how a person's personality traits make them more suited to some careers than others. She was well into her career before she realized that she prefers silence to noise, tranquility to action, tasks to talking. So she created exercises to help the kids identify their own personality traits, and they talked about what careers might fit.

Things were clicking along when Ms. McCullough happened to mention, as an aside, that as a freelance writer and editor she works from home. She mentioned that she now shares an office with her golden retriever who is a quiet, but congenial, office mate. Suddenly, hands shot up all over the room.

And they were off.

"Ms. McCullough, I have a dog, her name is Abbey, and she sleeps with me."

"Ms. McCullough, my mom took our dog to the vet, and it got x-rayed, because it ate a *sock*."

"Ms. McCullough, we have a yellow lab, and it steals our *underwear*!"

Kids who had previously looked drowsy or bored, suddenly perked up, too, frantically waving their hands in the air.

And in an instant it all came rushing back, déjà vu of hundreds of lessons, when your intention to take a class discussion one way is hijacked in completely unexpected directions. And try as you might to hold on, to bring it back, it's like trying to give a cat a bath. Soon you're as bedraggled as the cat.

"Okay, let's get back to careers," she said. "Who can tell me—"

The bell rang and kids filed out. Several stopped. A line formed, each waiting their turn, she was sure, to tell her how much they learned from the stimulating presentation.

"Ms. McCullough, my dog, Tiny, tried to run away and he was *pulling his dog house behind him*!"

"Ms. McCullough, my dog Trixie, got into the litter box and *ate cat poop!*"

"Ms. McCullough, we have a dog named Magnolia, and she farts *really bad*! My mom calls her *Fart Blossom*!"

Sigh. Every dog has his day.

This wasn't hers.

LIFE IN THE FISHBOWL

It's not easy to conduct business in a fishbowl. From the outside looking in, things get distorted. Refracted. Magnified.

That's part of the reason school districts so zealously guard information about discipline incidents. The court of public opinion is one tough lady. The other reason, of course, is that individual student discipline records are protected by the Family Educational Rights and Privacy Act (FERPA).

But according to Mr. Dooley, an assistant principal approaching his fortieth year in the public school system, students and parents alike have become high maintenance. So high, in fact, that many districts spend the majority of their resources on student behavior.

Parents and grandparents used to teach citizenship at home, Mr. Dooley says. Even the church had more influence over student behavior. Now school districts must pick up the slack, and it's taking its toll in countless ways. Discipline hassles have soared, not just in the number of incidents each day, but in the length of time it takes to process them.

A half hour spent handling a simple discipline referral is now often followed by three or four hours of arguing with parents. They want the names and phone numbers of every student who witnessed the incident, and they want the teacher put on trial. If they don't get their way at the building level they take it to central administration, wasting time and resources there, too.

Sometimes parents campaign for justice by gathering support from other parents. Sometimes, they go so far as to take their story to the media. Once that happens, the school district almost always ends up looking bad because per FERPA, they walk a legal minefield if they try to defend their actions.

In schools all across the nation administrators sag under the weight of almost overwhelming discipline problems that have reached epic proportions on the drama scale.

Lunchtime Fridays often mean standing room only in the main office, as kids wait to be disciplined. And principals spend many mornings sorting out disputes that happened on the buses on the way in to school. Nothing is black and white and it takes the wisdom of Solomon to be fair and still maintain a consistent discipline policy.

Too often, what should be a simple discipline decision gets snarled when an angry student with an attitude escalates a simple infraction into a full-blown confrontation.

So why do so many parents side with their children when they misbehave? Many parents, according to Mr. Dooley, are having their own battles with their kids. If parents go to bat for them it can buy them a bit of peace and tranquility. There's an unspoken agreement that says, "If I get you out of trouble at school, you'd better do what I ask at home."

It's not only resources, though, that are drained. Faculty and staff are, too. Mr. Dooley believes that in the future there will be very few thirty- to forty-year career educators because to serve parents and students in this way takes a high level of energy that is emotionally, mentally, and physically demanding. And it never lets up. No hour of the day, no day of the week, no week of the school year offers relief.

It's a thankless job to be a principal. And it's hard to focus on leadership and teaching and learning while mediating the murky and the absurd.

But the rules in a school, which are put in place to maintain a serious learning environment and keep kids safe, take another hit every time a parent overturns a discipline decision. And once an allowance has been made for one student, there's a feeding frenzy as students, and yes, their parents, work every angle.

School discipline used to be about gum chewing or running in the hall. And the student was always guilty, in actuality or not. It may not always have been fair, but at least it was simple.

The truth is, things would be much more tolerable in the fishbowl, if only people would quit tapping on the glass.

POPCORN, A DIPLOMA, AND A LARGE COKE, PLEASE

Be careful what you wish for.

Parents that complain that they aren't given enough tickets to their child's graduation ceremony, or that the school auditorium is uncomfortably small, may find themselves attending graduation in a sports arena. And once that happens, this solemn, stately event loses every bit of its pomp.

Being jammed into a small auditorium has some advantages. For one thing, there's a certain amount of accountability when people sit close. A person who talks is likely to be shushed by the person who wants to hear the speech. And no one gets up and moves around because there's nowhere to go.

Not so for graduations held in sports arenas.

In a circus-like atmosphere complete with nachos, air horns, cowbells, and a hot almond stand, many guests come simply to socialize. They wander in late, talk, laugh, and walk the stands looking for friends. After sitting in one spot for a while, they get up and move to a different seat. They come to see and be seen, and anything happening on the dais below takes second stage to that.

If the auditorium allows too few guests, the arena allows too many. From the principal's opening remarks to the last hurrah, few in the audience pay attention. Kids run free, cell phones chirp, and people in jeans and tennis shoes climb up and down stairs balancing buckets of popcorn and jumbo Cokes. Even the broom crew is out in force, constantly sweeping up after the litterbugs.

The crowd starts out restless and gets worse. Apparently no one can go two hours without a snack, and the length of the line at the concession stand grows in direct proportion to the length of the speeches.

Constant chatter and movement make it hard to pay attention, but some try. On either side of the dais, closest to the graduates, parents and family listen intently. They arrived early to get what passes for a good seat in a gigantic warehouse. Their hands hold cameras instead of hot pretzels, but unfortunately, without a telephoto lens they're still too far away to get a decent photo of their child's magic moment. Still, they do their best to be engaged in the ceremony.

The rest of the crowd is superfluous. The worst offenders are other students. It would be nice to think they were there for inspiration, to contemplate their own graduation.

But no. Groups of teenagers, clad in baseball caps, sunglasses perched on top, skulk around texting on smartphones. They ignore the speakers until they hear applause, chime in with a fist pump and a guttural, "Yeah!" and promptly go back to texting. And because it's such a big place, they're anonymous. There's no one to tell them to behave.

School officials work hard to put on a well-orchestrated, dignified ceremony, in spite of the setting and some of the guests. But let's face it; if a ceremony is held in a sports arena, people behave like they're at a sporting event. All sense of decorum is lost. Any family looking for an intimate experience will be sadly disappointed.

Schools move their graduations to sports arenas because stepfamilies and extended families are too large for high school gymnasiums and auditoriums. And like many innovations, it probably seemed like a good idea at the time. But they'll either have to adjust to graduation under the big top, or move it back to school and limit the tickets.

Forget about pomp and circumstance.

In an arena, it's just chomp and circulate.

PAYING THE PRICE

We're all guilty. Everyone's done it. We've all scoffed in envy at the salary, vacation, or perks of one profession or another.

Like professional athletes, for example. It's hard to fathom why they earn such exorbitant salaries for simply throwing a fastball or slam dunking a basketball.

Ah, but teacher pay. Now there's kindling for a firestorm of debate.

For teachers, there are days that are so much fun it's hard to believe they get paid to do it. And there are days when they leave the building thinking there isn't enough money in the world to make them go back.

That teacher that you see grading papers in the waiting room of the doctor's office will not be rid of the weight of that pile of papers until June. The pile never grows smaller because there's always a new assignment. And if they get even a bit behind that pile has the potential to get so big so fast, they fantasize about it catching fire and turning to ash.

That teacher will grade a few papers here and there all evening, squeezing in a few while the pasta is boiling, during TV commercials, or at their own child's soccer game.

At the end of first marking period, Ms. Cleary, a sophomore English teacher, has graded 4,872 assignments. Her average grading time is five minutes per assignment, twenty minutes for essays, to less than a minute for easy stuff. She has spent a total of seventeen days outside of school grading.

In addition to the family time that is sacrificed while grading papers, she spends part of the family budget to maintain her certification. After earning her bachelor's degree and paying tuition to student teach for a semester, unpaid, she paid for fingerprinting and a background check by the FBI, a basic skills test, tests in her major and minor, and her provisional certificate which is good for six years.

When she landed a teaching job, she became responsible for fifteen days of professional development (beyond what the district requires) in the first three years, at her own expense. She must also acquire eighteen credit hours (at $350–$475 per credit hour) to get her professional certificate, and pay for both. Then she must take six credits every five years at her own expense, for the rest of her career. Add to that the cost of books, gas for out-of-town classes, and parking.

It costs a lot to be a teacher.

Some believe that if teachers were paid less, there could be more money spent on students. But one look at states where teachers are poorly paid and it's clear that's a fallacy. They still have old, out-of-date buildings and the same budget problems all schools face.

People who have decided that teachers are overpaid and underworked rarely change their minds. But consider this: Forty percent of all new teachers leave within three years.

So if it's really such a cake job, why aren't people waiting in line to be hired?

HELLO, SECRETARY?

Brrring!

"OK class, that was the tardy bell. We'll begin discussing the Progressive Era right after I take attendance. Open your books to chapter 19. . . I'll just enter this into the attendance book for the state. . . and then enter it into the computer for the office. . . Okay, all set. Now. . ."

"Yo, Ms. Flynn, I know I'm late, but honest, it wasn't my fault. . ."

"Adam, this is your fourth tardy. I don't have a choice. The Student Handbook clearly states that students are to be referred to the office on the fourth tardy. Wait while I write up this discipline referral. . . There. Take this and go to the office. OK, class, as you know, the Progressive Era took place in. . . Oops, I almost forgot, Bobby and Joe, you need to sign the athletic eligibility to acknowledge that I verbally told you that you are ineligible to play this week. Sign right here. Okay, where were we? Ah yes, the Progressive Era. . ."

"Ms. Flynn, I need this field trip permission slip signed."

"Trina, I already signed your permission slip."

"I know, but I lost that one and I had to get a new one. Pleeease, sign it so I can go?!"

"Later Trina. We're in the middle of class here. Okay, when you read the chapter on the Progressive Era you learned. . ."

Knock, knock, knock.

"Ms. Flynn, I'm going home sick and my mom's on her way to pick me up. The lady in the office told me to go see all of my teachers and get my homework."

"Sally, I'm in the middle of class here. . . "

"But I need my work *now*. My mom won't have the car later to come up and get it."

"Okay. Just a minute. Class, start the questions at the end of the chapter. OK, Sally, here you go. Now. Who can tell me what the Progressive Era. . ."

Knock, knock, knock.

"Ms. Flynn, the principal would like to see Josh Williams in his office right away."

"Josh, they need you in the office. . . OK, where were we?"

"Ms. Flynn, what did we do last week? I was in Florida."

"Joe, you'll have to see me after class, we're in the middle of—"

"I don't got time after class, I got to get all the way upstairs to math class after this!"

"I'll talk to you at the end of the hour, Joe. Now, where were we?"

"MAY I HAVE YOUR ATTENTION. MAY I HAVE YOUR ATTENTION PLEASE, FOR A VERY IMPORTANT ANNOUNCEMENT."

"Shhhh, class, listen, this sounds important."

"STUDENTS WHO ARE GOING ON THE HUMANITIES FIELD TRIP NEED TO REPORT TO THE FLAGPOLE IMMEDIATELY. I REPEAT, STUDENTS WHO ARE GOING ON THE HUMANITIES FIELD TRIP NEED TO REPORT TO THE FLAGPOLE IMMEDIATELY."

"OK, if you're going on that field trip raise your hand so I can find your name on this list. When I find your name you may leave. Okay. . .done. Now, let's get down to work. . ."

"Hey, Ms. Flynn, you know I got, like, permission to leave early, right, 'cause we got, like, this cross country meet today and the team gots to be on the bus by 1:30. You got the notice on that, right?"

"Let me just check the list, Billy, and make sure you're on it. Yep, you can leave at 1:30. . . "

Knock, knock, knock.

"Ms. Flynn, would you please pass out these overdue library slips to the appropriate students?"

"Oh, right. Thank you. OK class, what did you learn about the Progressive Era?"

Brrring!

Sigh.

And people wonder why test scores aren't higher.

READING, WRITING, AND RETAINERS

"We have nothing to fear but fear itself," according to Franklin Roosevelt.

Obviously ol' Frank has never worked in a twenty-first century public school system, because there's a lot to be afraid of.

Namely, lawsuits.

When dealing with the entire stratum of society, life can get a little nutty. Just when one thinks they've heard it all, something comes along that tops it. And for administrators, that nuttiness translates into an almost manic fear of lawsuits.

Every thought, every decision, every move they make is run through a mental lawsuit meter which attempts to determine how the decision will stand up in court. The lawsuit meter is second only to the press meter, which tries to determine how the decision will look if it ends up splashed across the front page of a newspaper.

All school personnel fear lawsuits, so they constantly second-guess themselves and the big and small decisions they make.

"Okay, Johnny, that's the fifth time I've caught you writing on your desk. I'll see you at lunch and you can clean all of the desks in the room."

But wait.

Will this scar Johnny for life? Will he grow up to have a cleaning phobia and come back ten years from now and sue me? Will he turn into a child abuser, making his own children clean repeatedly? Is this humiliating to him? Will the other kids tease him for it, and if they do, will he lash out violently and perhaps get a gun and shoot us all?

What if he develops a rash from the cleaning spray? What if he gets a headache from the smell? What if he develops cleaning elbow and it ruins his potential for a career in professional sports?

Is it worth the risk, or should I just clean this desk myself?

So here is the prediction: In the very near future every school will have a lawyer on staff. Not a lawyer on retainer, as they currently do. They'll hire full-time lawyers and give them an office right next to the principal's. Teachers will have the lawyer's number on speed dial and every time they have a question they'll dial him up.

"Uh, Mr. Lawyer, my students are doing a social studies project that requires them to trace their family trees. . ."

"No, Mr. Teacher, you can't require them to do that, because kids who have unsavory characters in their lineage may be embarrassed."

Or, "Ms. Lawyer, I think I'm in trouble. I put Johnny's A+ essay on the bulletin board and now his mother is angry because the kids are calling him a nerd."

"You're right, Ms. Teacher, you are in trouble. You need to take measures to fix this immediately. Write a letter of apology to Johnny and his mother. Maybe we can nip this one in the bud."

You laugh, but these examples are real.

The fact is that fear-based decisions are not good decisions. But lawsuits are costly, time-consuming, and they bring negative press, three things school districts can't afford.

And the best offense is a good defense, right?

AS SAFE AT SCHOOL AS ANYWHERE

One winter day a year after the Columbine massacre, Ms. Berg was teaching her fourth hour class when one of her students pointed out the window and shouted cheerfully, "Hey look! It's a bum!"

She looked and, sure enough, right outside the classroom window was a scruffy man wearing a ragged coat, carrying a lumpy brown paper bag.

Immediately half the kids jumped up and headed for the window, laughing and pointing as if it were a circus act.

Ms. Berg processed the information from a different point of view:

"Dirty scruffy guy, don't know who he is, never saw him before, what's he got in the bag, danger, danger DANGER!"

"Get away from that window this minute!" she hissed. "Get over by the door right now!"

Every kid froze, shocked by her tone of voice.

She called the office, keeping her eye on the guy and the kids. Eventually, security arrived. It turned out that he was, indeed, a homeless man, and the security guard escorted him off school grounds.

The students forgot the incident as quickly as it happened.

Ms. Berg did not.

Over the next few days she thought a lot about "What if. . ."

What if he had a hammer in the bag and used it to break the window and get at the kids? What if he had a gun? What if he had a bomb? What if, what if, *what if?*

It's a testament to our optimism that school districts haven't turned their buildings into prisons in an effort to make them safer. Most people think something like Columbine won't happen at their school. But it's important in times of crisis to feel like you're doing something, anything, and so with limited budgets districts have done what they can.

One cheap and easy step toward peace of mind is to issue identification badges to staff members. But how effective are they, really? Even in a large school most staff members recognize each other, even if they can't recall their name. And if the intention is to delineate staff from outsiders, it's crucial that everyone wear the ID badges at all times. Yet they don't.

Most schools started locking all outside doors except one. They were careful about it at first, too. But gradually, fear recedes and things get lax. Doors are left open and untended. Today it's the door where the food is delivered. Tomorrow it's the loading dock. The next day Johnny sticks a rock in the door to leave it open for his friend.

Nonschool personnel walk in and out of schools all day. Signs posted on the doors encourage visitors to check in at the office, and the good and honest people gladly do. Someone intent on doing harm, of course, will not.

Smaller buildings and smaller student populations allow school personnel to keep better tabs on things, yet the trend for upsizing buildings continues. And in a large building with a large student population, there are literally dozens of places to hide—a person, a weapon, or a bomb.

Surveillance cameras may be helpful, but would they have helped at Columbine? No. Dylan Klebold and Eric Harris were intent on a grand massacre and were willing to die in the process. What would they care about a camera?

Lockdown drills accustom kids to the idea of huddling on the floor under a table or behind a filing cabinet. But the TV generation can imagine every possible scenario: "Ms. Berg, what if the guy comes through the window, not the door? What if he's already hiding in your back room and we don't know it and we're locked in with him? What if he just shoots off the lock?" they ask.

Ms. Berg doesn't have the answers.

Like it or not our security—in schools and in society—is not necessarily something we can assure, regardless of what the director of Homeland Security or the local superintendent says.

So are schools any more secure today than they were before Columbine? Yes.

About as secure as our borders and airports since 9/11.

And that's not exactly comforting.

HEADY WITH HORSEPOWER

"Be especially careful when driving past a bar," the driver's training teacher admonishes. "People are apt to pull out without looking."

Ironically, the same advice holds true for people driving past high schools on warm afternoons in the spring. Because nowhere is spring celebrated more exuberantly than in the parking lot of a high school.

The first brush of warm air has kids bursting from the building with the bell, young men stripping off shirts, warm sun on skinny, winter white chests. Out come the phones (who are they *texting*?) and on go the caps. Some carry backpacks, but many do not (no homework?), arms swinging loose and free.

A strut to the car, look at me, hoots and hollers, heys and high fives. Cars are still parked haphazardly from the morning rush to first hour, when kids created parking spots where there are none.

"Come on, I'll give you a ride!" kids yell to anyone and everyone, any excuse just to stay in this car a little longer, windows down, eardrums aching with the thumping, jumping, bumping music that defines them. To see and be seen through the anonymity of sunglasses, letting the choice of music tell their story.

The cars are much nicer now than they were in the days of the jalopies, and more kids have them, but there's still variety, from the beater to the sublime. Kids' lives revolve around long hours at menial jobs to pay for those wheels if Mom and Dad won't foot the bill.

As June draws close the high jinks get wilder, and sunning on the roofs of cars turns to dancing on the roofs of cars.

More expansive in the parking lot than they would ever be inside the school, the unlikeliest of kids talk to each other. In the safety and familiarity of their cars they casually light up, looking authority in the eye, daring someone to bust them.

It's the meeting place, the show-off place, and on weekends occasionally the party place, judging by the brown bottles that roll through on Monday morning.

With school personnel at a premium it's usually the least patrolled place too, resulting in theft, vandalism, and the dealing of drugs.

When they finally leave, it's jackrabbit starts and the irresistible tire squeal—"Look at me! Look at me!" fast and careless, heady with horse power.

The downside of such exuberance is the regularity of fender benders, in the parking lot and in front of the school, inexperienced drivers dazed by the hot sun and their own cool.

And though the morning parking lot is busy too, the mood is frantic not buoyant, simply a mad dash of sleepy kids racing to beat the bell.

So if bad timing puts you in front of a high school at dismissal, roll down your windows, crank up your radio, put on your sunglasses and recapture your youth.

Just make sure you drive defensively.

THE SHUFFLED CHILDREN

They are The Shuffled Children.

Every teacher knows them. Actually, every teacher knows a lot of them. And for every shuffled child they know of in their classes, there are a dozen more that they aren't aware of.

You know some Shuffled Children, too. They're the kids who are shuffled back and forth between their estranged parents' houses several times a week.

Sometimes these kids know the shuffle-schedule. Other times they don't know for sure where they will be on any given night.

The Shuffled Children may not have a time or place where they can get their homework done. Often they spend evenings with a parent running errands or visiting relatives. They might try to study for a test in the car. Quite often they come to school without their backpacks or other materials, having left them at one parent's house or the other.

Sometimes they can't get the backpack until the next time they see that parent. It frustrates teachers when the child doesn't have his schoolwork. But not having his schoolwork is the least of this kid's worries.

Teachers are never sure which parent to call when there's a problem. And they get conflicting stories when they finally do reach a parent. Sometimes one parent expresses frustration or anger with the other parent's parenting. This makes the teacher uncomfortable. It makes the child even more uncomfortable.

The Shuffled Children might have two bedrooms, one at each parent's house. The rules at each might be different. This is confusing to the child. But they'll take advantage of it if they can.

There are other kinds of Shuffled Children, too. Like the ones who are shuffled from one living situation to another. It's an old story; Mom moves in with her boyfriend, or Dad moves in with his girlfriend, and the child has to move, too. It doesn't work out, so they move again. Eventually she meets a new guy, he meets a new girl, and they believe once again that this is The One. But it's not. So they move. Again.

Sometimes the new boyfriend or girlfriend has kids, too. Suddenly, there are two sets of kids sharing bedrooms, bathrooms and most importantly, their parent, with virtual strangers, day in and day out. Often these households don't have any kind of schedule or routine. Basically, it's every kid for himself. There aren't many Brady Bunch moments. The kids may or may not like Mom or Dad's new friend. After all, they don't even know them, do they?

No one asks the kids how they feel about all this. No one prepares them for it. This huge lifestyle change makes them sad and scared and angry. It's hard to concentrate at school when you're worried about what happens after school, or where you'll sleep tonight. Eventually, out of anger and frustration, The Shuffled Children act up in class.

This moving from one living situation to another often involves a change of school district. So not only is the child shuffled, but their transcripts are shuffled, too. In some urban districts, by June the teachers have almost none of the same kids they started with in September.

Sometimes the child moves into and out of the same school district several times. Teachers and office workers do the paperwork for the check-out process, only to do it again when the child re-enrolls a few months later.

Sometimes moving makes the children miss important material in class. Sometimes they get the same material twice. But once again, schoolwork is the least of their worries. After all, they have to make new friends, learn new routines, find their way around new buildings, bus routes and classes. Their new teachers have new rules and procedures. That's a lot of scary new stuff to learn. Who has time to worry about schoolwork?

Unless they happen to be unusually resilient, the world doesn't feel like a safe place to The Shuffled Children. How could it, when their home life can change on a whim?

The Shuffled Children.

It's not their fault.

STILL NO GIRLS ALLOWED

Mothers, take heed: The Good Ol' Boys Club is alive and well in your daughter's school.

And she's still being left out of it.

Ms. Daly has been advising student publications for fourteen years, working closely with the same group of students for four years at a stretch in a teamlike setting.

For some reason, the publications class is typically made up of mostly girls. Ms. Daly comes from a family of girls, too, no brothers or boy cousins. So it's a bit of a culture shock for her the first time she has a staff with a large number of boys. Locker room jokes and roughhousing aside, she discovers that the good ol' boys' instinct is as natural to them as breathing.

She watches, amazed. The least talented of the group are treated by the other boys as if they are stars, and the most talented as if they are gods. Backslapping and high-fiving, they sing each other's praises endlessly. One of them might be an absolute twit, but if he is part of the club, he is golden. And the twits, thanks to their buddies, will probably pull six-figure salaries someday.

If she comes down on one of the boys the rest of the group jumps to his defense, sighing, eye rolling, and arguing. As a mere female, her opinion is as insignificant to them as the other girls'.

Private jokes and insider stories prevail, to the exclusion of everyone else. Forget about staff teamwork. They are their own team.

Don't misunderstand. Ms. Daly likes these boys. They are funny and smart and basically kind. But it's an eye-opener, this up-close-and-personal look at how the Good Ol' Boys Club works. And she had no idea how early it starts. She also didn't know how completely left out of it girls are. Girls who are twice as talented as the boys are often cowed by them.

For better or worse, the girls just don't have the camaraderie or unity. Rarely do they compliment each other or stick up for each other. Around the boys, they don't stick up for themselves, either.

The women's movement seems to have bypassed girls in a number of ways. Things that were de rigueur to Ms. Daly growing up in the 1970s are a mystery to her students.

For example, Ms. Daly decided early on that she would keep her maiden name when she married. It is not a political statement. Just a very strong sense of self. She also doesn't wear a wedding ring, though she is happily married. These two topics absolutely confound her female students year after year. Every time a new group of students figures out that her husband is the history teacher down the hall with the different last name, they scratch their heads in wonder.

"But why don't you want people to know you're married?" the girls ask. "Is it a secret?" Or, "What's with this 'Ms.' thing anyway?" Inevitably this is followed with, "When I get married I *want* to take my husband's last name. . . and he'd *better* buy me a really big ring!"

Ms. Daly's explanation about being your own person while sharing your life with another falls on deaf ears. They just don't get it.

In some ways, women's lib seems to have missed the mark. Girl Power seems to be more about the right to dress slutty than about true empowerment. Teen magazines encourage girls to "be themselves," but only in reference to the clothes they wear or the hairstyles they choose.

Granted, the women's movement and Title IX have ensured that girls will be allowed to take woodshop (at her high school in 1972 Ms. Daly could not) and have the same athletic teams the boys have. But forty years later, Ms. Daly just doesn't see the kind of fundamental change in girls that she hoped for.

How would empowerment look on a teenage girl? Decisive. Assertive. Independent. Supportive of other girls.

Moms, talk to your girls. Just saying, "You can be anything you want to be when you grow up," is not enough. Tell them that they are strong. Tell them that when they boost other girls they don't detract from themselves. Tell them that they don't need to look for their self-worth in the eyes of a boy.

Tell them to form their own damn club.

SEARCHING FOR A FEMALE ROLE MODEL

Quick, list three positive role models for young girls.

Okay, now try it again, only this time, don't include any athletes.

Pretty tough, huh?

Now list three not-so-positive role models for girls. Bet that was much easier, wasn't it?

It seems that everywhere we turn there are examples of how we don't want young girls to be. The world of sports has some exceptions with strong role models in the WNBA, college athletics, and the Olympics.

But what about girls who don't play sports?

Betty Friedan, author of *The Feminine Mystique* and the first president of the National Organization for Women, freed women of the notion that they had to be homemakers. She advocated that women could have interests other than husbands and families and should aspire to separate identities.

Over forty years later, it's a message that girls still need to hear.

A surprising number of girls have never heard of the National Organization for Women, the Equal Rights Amendment, or the Constitutional Equality Amendment. Somewhere along the line we dropped the ball and too many girls still believe that the boy is the prize, a concept that's reinforced by silly young women fighting over one man on reality television shows like *The Bachelor*. Fistfights between girls at school are almost always over a boy. And way too many girls are still willing to change their friends, their looks, their personality, and their interests, for a boy.

Unfortunately, many examples of young womanhood today are not accomplished or wholesome. And that's the rub. The ones we would choose to be our daughters' role models are not necessarily who they would choose for themselves. While baby boomers listened to their moms talk about Betty Friedan and Gloria Steinam, too many girls today aspire to be Justin Beiber's girlfriend.

Still, we have to try. If girls prefer the vapid half-dressed pop stars writhing on music videos, we need to counter the image with examples of substance. Jessica Simpson may be a business tycoon, but that's not why girls emulate her.

Part of the problem is that we only give girls half the message. "You can be anything you want" we say, and leave it at that. We need to have the entire conversation, including some good strong examples of what they could be. We need to show them how to get there. We need to, somehow, make them hear the message that, yes, boys are nice, but they're the icing, not the cake.

The next time you chat with a young girl, don't ask her if she has a boyfriend or tell her that she's pretty. Instead, ask her what she's proud of, what she's good at, what she wants to do with her life, and how she plans to make a difference in the world.

Girls who believe that the boy is the prize lose the real prize: themselves. Teach girls to quit looking to boys for validation. Teach girls to put their own interests first.

Teach girls to tell boys, unequivocally, "I've got things to do. But you're welcome to come along for the ride."

'Twas the Day Before Break

'Twas the day before break, and all through the school
Not a student was working, most behaving like fools.
DVDs were cued up, kids played learning games,
In hopes that the chaos could somewhat be tamed.

The children were buzzing from sugar and glee,
Anticipation mounting for the next two weeks free.
And I and my nerves, or what little was left
Had finally sat down, bemused and bereft.

When out in the hall there arose such a clatter,
I sprang from my desk to see what was the matter.
Away to the door, thinking, "Oh God, what now?"
Threw it wide open, expecting a row.

The light from the window at the end of the hall
Framed the silhouette of men, some short and some tall.
My wondering eyes saw a crazy sideshow,

A state politician with eight yes-men in tow.

With a perfect white smile so dazzling and slick,
I knew in a moment, it was political shtick.
Most rapid with handshakes, he cruised down the hall
A publicity ploy was the gist of it all.

"Now, test scores, Now merit pay, Now vouchers for all!
Oh funding, Oh tax cuts, Oh budget shortfall.
I'll save education, I tell you, I will
If you'll only help send me to Capitol Hill!"

As campaign leaflets before an election do fly,
The truth and straight answers were in short supply.
So up to the main office, the yes-men, they flew
With an agenda of promises and the politician, too.

And then in a twinkling, I saw from afar
The smiling glad-handing of the self-proclaimed star.
As I drew back my hand and was turning to hide
Down the hall came the press corp. with cameras held wide.

The Rep. was all dressed in his suit and matched tie
This orchestrated photo-op would not pass him by.
A bundle of laptops he had flung on his back,
And he looked like a fence just opening his pack.

His eyes, how they scanned each one for approval
Hecklers were targeted for early removal.
His droll little mouth which spoke only swill,
Begged our support for his education bill.

"Per pupil funding must be slashed," so he said.
"Merit awards and laptops, you'll get instead.
So we cut adult ed., didn't need it anyhow
But don't touch my salary, that's a sacred cow."

He preened and he postured, a self-righteous old elf
And I gagged when I saw him in spite of myself.
A wink of his eye and a nod of his head,
Soon gave me to know I had everything to dread.

He spoke without stopping, full of rhetoric was he
"The Report Cards are coming, failing schools cannot be!
I'll save education! The schools I can fix!
But input from teachers we'll just have to nix."

He sprang to his Towncar, to his cronies he waved,

And away they all sped, another school to be saved.
But I heard him exclaim, "Keep this in mind—
With me at the helm there's no child left behind!"

SUMMER, SWEATY SUMMER

Step inside, and the smelly, steamy heat slaps you like a wet sweat sock. To an unsuspecting visitor, it's disconcerting. Shocking. But those on the inside know that the first hot spell in late May turns schools into sweat boxes and students into zombies.

Sleepy, heavy-lidded, glazed and dazed students droop across their desks. Small classroom windows stand wide open, letting in better-than-nothing air. Sans screens, they're an open invitation to equally somnolent bees, whose buzzing appearance jars kids into dramatic squeals of terror.

In desperation, teachers turn off classroom lights, hoping to lower the temperature a degree or two, or at least give that impression. Some students fan themselves furiously, raising their temperature even more.

The groundskeeper zips by, open throttle, clad in headphones and sunglasses, tractor engine stunningly loud under the window, but bringing some relief with the fresh scent of cut grass. If your students don't have allergies the windows can be left open, and it's heaven.

There's no nice way to say it—the halls smell, like people unfamiliar with deodorant or soap. You can't escape the smell, either: It's everywhere, imprinted in your nose, clinging to your clothes, making you self-conscious and eager to hurry home and peel it away, straight into the washer.

Wilted teachers make excuses to hang around in air-conditioned offices during their planning hours, where secretaries and principals cheerfully work as fresh as they were upon arriving that morning.

It's a loose look teachers have adopted for the day, dressed for picnics rather than business, sandals, no socks, loose dresses, ponytails, even shorts, anything to catch a breath of breeze and release some body heat.

In spite of the lethargy, tempers are short and flare easily. Shiny-faced kids move through too-crowded halls, sticky elbow bumping sticky elbow, clammy skin on skin.

Cranky with heat, students beg to go outside or just put their heads down and sleep. A few brave teachers do take them outside, while other classes watch jealously from the sauna windows. Some kids feign work for fear of being dragged back inside, but most don't, giving themselves over to cool grass and blissful shade.

After school, teachers run to the store and spend their own money on fans for their classrooms, then Sharpie their names all over them, hoping they don't disappear overnight because they're too big to be locked up in cabinets.

The canned breeze is divine, in spite of the constant scramble to anchor papers on desks.

On these blistering days little work gets done, and the day feels pregnant with waiting. Unused to such discomfort, kids watch the clock, thinking of air-conditioning and popsicles and pools waiting at home; waiting for the last bell of the day, the last day of school.

The novelty of the heat wave wears off fast. Soon teachers scan the sky hopefully, looking for clouds, longing for rain.

For there's work yet to be done before that last bell of the year.

SILENCE THE NAME-CALLERS

Blow queen. Faggot. Cocksucker. Fudge packer. Butt pirate. Dick licker. Dyke. Lesbo.

Ugly words, aren't they? It's hard to write them, and no doubt hard to read them. Imagine, then, hearing those names and worse, hissed at you in the halls of your school every day.

That's the reality for thousands of gender nonconforming students as they struggle with their sexual identity in a mean, cold place called high school.

Remember high school? Remember worrying about fitting in, wearing the right clothes, having the right friends? Even popular students can be riddled with private insecurities.

Imagine, then, being a gender nonconforming student and keeping silent about a secret that, if known, would not only make you an outcast, but would so threaten some people that they beat you up, just for the sport of it.

And what if you couldn't talk to your parents about it? Where would you turn?

GLSEN, the Gay, Lesbian & Straight Education Network, works to create safe schools for all students. One way they do that is by working with educators to address anti-LGBT behavior and bias in schools, and to protect students from bullying and harassment. They also guide students and staff in establishing gay–straight alliances, student clubs where any student, straight or not, can go for information and support.

Gay–straight alliances do not promote homosexuality or encourage kids to be gay. They simply provide information and support for questioning students. They function much like any student club; kids speaking ordinary kid-speak, joking and laughing and fooling around, planning events and pro-crastinating like kids everywhere.

One powerful project that gay–straight alliances promote nationwide is the annual National Day of Silence. On this day hundreds of thousands of students take a vow of silence to bring attention to anti-LGBT name-calling, bullying, and harassment in their schools, passing out cards to explain their silence and to invite others to participate.

When asked what they get out of membership in this club, students answer without hesitation: "It's a sanctuary." "It fosters understanding." "We provide an example for the rest of the school." "We can help educate people." "We can learn."

And there it is: Education. Gay–straight alliances offer questioning students solid information from reliable sources. Without that, vulnerable students turn to unsavory characters in Internet chat rooms, and fall into negative gay stereotypes of promiscuity, drugs and even suicide.

Being gay is not a choice. But education is. We can always choose to open our minds and learn. And these brave kids will teach us.

Every April, youth across the country wear T-shirts and pass out cards in an effort to educate students and support safe schools and equality for all people, regardless of sexual orientation and gender identity or expression. Their hope is that this positive, collective and audible silence will be the first step toward fighting harassment and prejudice.

And that eventually, the name-callers will be silenced forever.

ONLY IN OUR DREAMS

Oh, sweet victory.

Out they came, swaggering, strutting, heads held high. They were the best and they knew it. This victory against their rival team was hard won. They'd fought and scrabbled for every point. Privately they'd worried that they wouldn't be able to pull it off, but Coach assured them they were ready, and Coach was always right.

Hours, days, weeks of practice had finally paid off, and the state semifinal contest was over. Now they were headed for the championships, hoping, wishing, and fervently dreaming of that state title. Still wearing team colors, they filed into the hall where cheering fans and the press waited. The throng surged forward and surrounded them.

"You handled the pressure so well. How did you prepare?" asked a reporter from Channel 5.

"Well we've got Coach Fisher to thank for that. He took us through every conceivable scenario, so we were ready for anything," said Robbie, team captain. Thick blond hair fell over his forehead and he pushed it out of his eyes self-consciously.

"Robbie, Robbie, over here! WABC-TV! Can you tell us what was going through your mind in the final minutes?"

"I just knew if we could pick up those last points it would seal the victory for us," he said.

Reporters crowded around, a mass of bright lights and microphones. Fans too, tried to get the attention of their favorite competitor. Everyone wanted to be close to the team, to say they were there and they knew them when.

When they arrived at school the next day, balloons and posters covered their lockers. "Hometown Hero" glitter-penned in loopy letters. All day congratulations and high fives came from kids they didn't even know. Even teachers paused in their lessons to comment on the victory.

"Hey, way to go last night!"

"You were smokin'!"

"You totally trounced them, they didn't stand a chance!"

"You guys made them look like *babies!*"

Tickets to the championship were as hard to come by as tickets to a Jimmy Buffett concert. Principal O'Brian finally announced that they would be sold by lottery. Everyone grumbled, but the principal maintained that it was the only fair way. Lines for the lottery wound all the way down the hall at lunch.

On game day, kids eagerly crowded into the gym, to the special assembly being held in the team's honor. Stomping, screaming, they cheered themselves hoarse, feeling as if the team's victory was their victory, impressed and awed by their heroes.

Heads filled with game strategy, the team was nevertheless able to enjoy the moment and rise to the occasion.

Student frenzy. Community enthusiasm. Statewide attention. Pride. Recognition. Prestige. Scholarship buzz.

All this, because the state title was within reach. . .so close they could feel it. . .the highest honor possible. . .

For the Quiz Bowl Team.

Wait a minute—*what?*

Mental prowess prized as much as physical prowess?

Only in our dreams.

Chapter Five

Policy

From failing schools and merit pay to quirky brilliance and cleavage

Everyone is a genius. But if you judge a fish on its ability to climb a tree, it will live its whole life believing that it is stupid.

—Albert Einstein

IS MY SCHOOL REALLY FAILING?

Come inside.

Meet the people at this Phase 5 school, also known as a "failing" school because it has not made adequate yearly progress under the requirements of the federal No Child Left Behind Act (NCLB).

This school has a 47 percent mobility rate. That's the number of students transferring into and out of a school in a given year. High mobility rates correlate with low achievement rates because for students who move often, the curriculum is disrupted. They tend to have poor attendance and without intervention, these kids are likely to become drop-out statistics.

Though it's kept quiet, 10 to 15 percent of the families are homeless. Not only are they not homeowners, they don't even have a place to rent. They stay with friends or relatives until they are asked to leave. Then they move on and bunk with another friend or relative, and then another, on and on in an ugly, vicious cycle.

The parents mostly fall into three categories: Grandparents raising their grandchildren, parents who had their children when they were fourteen or fifteen years old, and foster parents.

Many of the students start kindergarten not knowing their colors, numbers, or alphabet. Some don't even know their own names, having been called nicknames like "Boo" their entire lives. Many cannot pick their own name out of a list, let alone write it. Many have never seen a book. They have no understanding even of the left-to-right concept in reading.

Behavior is the number one problem here. As a fourth grade class is taught multiplication, it appears that the entire class has Attention Deficit Disorder. They wiggle and tap and tear their papers. Their eyes constantly roam around the room, looking for someone to poke or prod. They cannot focus and they cannot keep still.

They also cannot multiply.

Defiance is the word of the day, every day. Their lives are about street survival. School is inconsequential. Teachers tread carefully; how much can you prod a student before he rebels? "I'm not doing that and you can't make me."

Anger reigns. Fists are the only way they know to settle disputes, and they use them freely. The ones who won't fight must be closely guarded by teachers or their pencils and lunch money will be stolen.

Parents were invited to the school to learn strategies to help their children prepare for the state standardized test. After a great deal of begging and the promise of a free meal, six to ten parents finally showed up.

First, they had to be taught how to multiply.

Not only the students will be tested. During the weeks leading up to The Test, the staff will be tested too, because students will go out of their way to get into trouble and be suspended, to avoid having to take The Test.

During the math lesson, no fourth grader can figure out 63 times 2. Yet when students face The Test they will be asked questions such as, "Max is at the carnival. He wants to play the Ball Toss. When he tosses the ball, it will land in one of the numbered rings: 25, 50, or 100. In his first game, Max will toss six balls at the rings. What is the lowest score he could get if the ball always lands in a numbered ring?"

So, will this be the year they pass The Test?

What do you think?

NICE SCHOOLS

"Teachers don't care if their students learn."

"A principal can't run a school as efficiently as a CEO can."

"School districts do nothing to curb dropout rates."

"Other countries do a better job of educating their kids than we do."

Follow education news in the mainstream media, and the predominant message is all of the above. You might even wonder if it's true.

And that's no accident. Now that corporate reformers have their cash registers wedged in the door of the public school system, education reform is big business. And so all sorts of organizations, foundations, and "think tanks" have cropped up, spewing unsubstantiated "facts" and biased reports, with the sole goal of discrediting public education.

And believe this, they're good. Really good. They look official, keep their partisan leanings hidden, and adopt noble sounding names like The Heritage Foundation or StudentsFirst.

For those who don't know better it's easy to mistake their wishes for facts and their vision for common sense. It's easy to believe that our schools are a mess.

But they're not. Every state is full of marvelous districts where things hum happily along most every day. Kids learn, test scores are good, discipline incidents are few, and there's a fine feeling of family in the air.

The problem is that there are some really troubled school districts in this country, too, especially in large cities like New York, Los Angeles, Chicago, and Washington D.C.

Those districts have problems. Big problems. And they often appear to have lost control: Test scores are low, the drop-out rate is high, and discipline issues rule the day.

It doesn't take a genius to connect the dots, to look at the neighborhoods those schools are in and see that these problems are born of poverty. But legislators and corporate reformers don't want to hear about poverty. They pretend it doesn't exist. So "poverty" has become a catchall term, a throwaway term, so overused in reference to education that it's lost its power.

The word "poverty" has different connotations for people depending on their worldview. Some equate poverty with laziness. Some think poverty is a choice. And still others think no further than "there but for the grace of God go I."

Most legislators seem to view poverty as an unsolvable problem, too large, expensive, and thankless to tackle. It's much easier to blame low test scores and high drop-out rates on the school system. And so the current reform movement vilifies teachers and their unions.

But the problems in poverty-stricken areas are so pervasive that they cast a looming, dark shadow over all districts—even the good ones. When legislators talk about education reform, they lump all public schools together, which does a terrible disservice to thousands of truly effective districts.

The common sense approach would be to fix the parts that are broken, not condemn the whole thing. First, fund education fairly so that all schools have enough money, not just the ones in nice neighborhoods. Second, repair the crumbling buildings—they are an embarrassment in this land of plenty. Third, create social programs that help families work their way out of poverty.

Current education reform has opted to condemn the entire system rather than simply fixing the parts that are broken, which demonstrates a profound lack of imagination.

And if your kids attend one of the nice schools, you ought to be concerned about that.

WE THE PEOPLE

Perhaps the most controversial of all elected positions is that of the school board member. Though some school board members in some communities evoke abiding respect and admiration, school boards in some districts can be astoundingly unknowledgeable about teaching and learning and basic school operations.

All too often they come to the role with a self-professed love of kids, but no skills to back it up. Too often they run for office to satisfy a personal ego trip, using their school board stint as résumé fodder, or a steppingstone to something else. In worst case scenarios members are manipulative and secretive, following their own hidden agenda.

But.

Unbridled power is equally dangerous. And top-down management typically serves best only those at the top. Thus, because school boards answer to the voting public, they are an imperfectly perfect example of We the People. They participate in the sometimes-ungainly struggle to set standards for the community we want to create.

An effective school board provides checks and balances and advocates for the good of the community. And while it's true that sometimes they have no true wisdom to bring to the education conversation, neither do most of the suits in Washington. Congress is often as unskilled, uneducated, and misguided about education policy as the worst school board. Worse yet, they are often far removed from our communities, literally and figuratively, and don't know our people, culture, or neighborhoods.

A local school board does.

Diminishing revenue and increased federal and state regulations make the work of school board members more challenging than ever. It is serious, time-consuming work now, much more demanding than photo ops and award ceremonies.

Granted, it is sometimes hard to muster up much patience for the bumbling incompetence of some school board members. But the fact is, We the People are as responsible for a lousy school board as the members themselves. After all, we elect them.

There's no doubt about it—We the People can be an ugly process. Personalities and egos regularly get in the way of progress. Some people talk way too much. Some get their feelings hurt too easily. Some hold grudges. Some can't see the big picture.

But that's life. That's us.

We the People.

DOING THEMSELVES IN

It won't be test scores, unqualified teachers or the corporate agenda that will ultimately result in the demise of the public school system.

Nope. Lack of fortitude is what will do them in.

Ask a veteran teacher how administration has changed over the years, and they will tell you that their biggest gripe is that administrators don't back teachers. In years past, if a teacher sent a student to the office, almost without exception a principal would discipline that child, no questions asked.

For better or worse, those days are gone. Now, if a teacher sends a student to the office, the teacher is questioned about the incident as exhaustively as the kid. "Are you sure this is what you saw? What you heard? How it started?" Teachers say that this questioning even happens in front of students, further undermining their authority.

Granted, administrators are busier than ever, and understandably resent handling routine discipline that a teacher should handle. It's a valid complaint. Some teachers are too quick to send a child to the office rather than cultivate their own discipline strategies.

Gone, too, are the days of "If you get in trouble at school you'll get in more trouble at home." Parents are the true power players in the public school equation. And therein lies the problem. In our litigious society, parents are quick to threaten lawsuits, most of which are ridiculous. Yet administrators too often react reflexively, protectively, going to great lengths to keep the customer satisfied.

And know this: the customer is not the student. It's the parent.

Keeping parents happy is a matter of survival. An unhappy parent has options and may just take their child elsewhere. And in the game of state funding, students equal money.

Let's say a student steals a cell phone and gets caught. Parents argue that as long as he gives it back, he should go unpunished. Administrators go along to keep the parent happy, and make the problem disappear. But it's exactly that kind of insidious undermining of discipline procedures that creates an undisciplined student body. And disenfranchised teachers.

So this mission to keep the customer satisfied has dangerous side effects. It compromises discipline policies which ultimately compromise the learning environment. Parents who want more than an undisciplined student body, a weak learning environment and disenfranchised teachers will seek alternative schools anyway.

So inadvertently, unconsciously, with the best of intentions, by trying to save themselves, the school system is slowly doing itself in.

Public schools are under incredible scrutiny right now. This is not the time to relax standards for behavior. Now is the time for school boards and administrators to stand up to politicians, lawyers, and the loud minority of threatening parents.

This is the time for courage, not compromise.

POLITICIAN, SERVE THY PEOPLE

Pick a politician, any politician. Now—how well do they serve you? Because that's what they're elected to do, you know. *Serve you.* So, how do they stack up as public servants? Are you getting your money's worth?

It's hard to know. Political commercials are not only hard to stomach, they don't tell us anything real about a candidate, except perhaps how low he's willing to stoop to be elected. And often, politicians with the kind of money it takes to run a campaign really can't relate to the public they serve.

For teachers, it is infuriating that out-of-touch politicians have complete control over decisions that affect teachers' classrooms. Yet, other than stump speeches and photo ops, most political candidates never set foot in schools, and haven't since they were students themselves.

But education is fundamental to the success of a society. Education policy is one of the most significant things an elected official will ever do.

Simply analyzing student data and test scores doesn't cut it, though. Policy makers need to meet the kids, and the teachers, in the trenches. So, to prove they're highly qualified, all political candidates should be required to complete the P.R.E.P. Internship, aka, the Politician's Real Experience Primer.

Unpaid, of course.

Here's how it would work:

To qualify, aspiring politicians must take every grade level of state-mandated test in every subject. Their scores will be published in the newspaper, where they will be analyzed and compared to other candidates'. Didn't make adequate progress? Tough. No race to the top for you.

Once they've passed the state-mandated tests, they will enter a school district for one semester, much like a student teacher. No grandstanding allowed.

Because funding cuts in schools have a domino effect, the political intern will do a variety of jobs so they understand the impact of such cuts—work the cafeteria line, observe guidance counseling sessions, shadow the school nurse for a day.

Children's attitudes and behavior speak volumes about their home lives. To that end, political interns will spend one week with custodians cleaning the cafeteria after lunch and the bathrooms after school. The shocking waste of food and the rudeness of students will teach them a great deal about their constituents.

They will drive a school bus for a week and break up fights at the bus stop. This provides the added bonus of experiencing the condition of the roads in their district and seeing where and how their voters live.

They will prepare and deliver several units of state test preparation for each level—elementary, middle and high school. Papers, of course, must be graded at home at night.

They will sit through several long curriculum meetings and attend parent/teacher conferences, in a building with no air conditioning on a ninety-degree day. They will accommodate the requests of those parents, no matter how absurd, and answer to parents who threaten lawsuits, with no legal representation by their side. One week will be spent making home visits with social workers, solving family problems, and finding funding when necessary.

For the written portion of the internship, they will create a budget for a first-year teacher, with spouse and child, that includes finding the time and money for mandated graduate classes.

Politician as public servant?

Oh please. They don't know the meaning of the term until they've worked in a public school.

MODUS OPERANDI

Mr. DeMille has a confession to make.

He doesn't like school.

He was an average student most of his life, content to coast along with Bs and Cs and the occasional D.

When a subject piqued his interest he easily made A's. His mom understood this about him and, as long as he was polite to his teachers, she pretty much left him alone about his grades.

And then, ironically, he became a teacher.

He is one of the few teachers on his staff that does not have a master's degree. He has nearly forty graduate credits, but he just can't seem to muster up enough interest to actually get the degree. He found most of the grad classes he took to be dull and useless.

But here's the thing: He loves to learn.

When he's interested in something he heads to the library, checks out a dozen books on the subject, and systematically plows right through them. And though no one makes him, he takes notes on what he reads, instinctively, almost unconsciously, because it helps him learn.

He's also endlessly curious and has been known to question friends so persistently that his wife chides him about it (which speaks more to her Minnesotan reticence than any rudeness on his part, he's certain).

He just doesn't like to learn what someone else thinks he should learn on the timetable they think he should learn it. It makes him cranky.

Teachers wring their hands over students like him. States pass more rigorous graduation requirements to challenge students like him. And the federal government created No Child Left Behind and Race to the Top in an attempt to measure students like him, complete with a list of things to be learned and a test to see if he's learned them.

But the fact is this: Wringing hands, tougher requirements, and federal mandates for testing would not have made a difference with him. He is destined to be the learner that he is, going at his own speed, in his own way.

Just like thousands of other students.

And for those who think that it's the school's responsibility to somehow break through to students like him and make education fun, consider this: Right now thousands of students are being forever turned off to learning by weeks and weeks of test prep and drill, and test upon standardized test.

Maybe deep down in his heart of hearts, his dissatisfaction with teaching is that he can no longer justify a life spent trying to force someone to learn what they're not ready to learn.

He doesn't waste a minute, though, regretting the average grades he earned, the master's degree he didn't get, or the things he didn't learn in school.

There's no time. He's got to get to the library.

EDUCATING FOR A DAY? OR A LIFETIME?

When parents send their children off to school, of course they hope that they will learn the right answers.

But it's important that they learn to ask the right questions as well.

That's what's at the heart of a serious rift between policy makers, legislators, and educators in this country. It's also the reason that most education reform fails.

We don't agree on the purpose of education.

Corporate reformers want to dismantle public education, sell the pieces to the highest bidder, and ultimately increase their company's bottom line.

Big business believes that the purpose of education is to create a better worker. And to a certain extent that's true.

Legislators believe that the purpose of education is to score well on standardized tests and prepare for a four-year college. And the fact that some students don't have the desire, the smarts, or the money to go to a four-year college is irrelevant to those legislators.

If the purpose of a K–12 education is to prepare all students for college, an initiative being promoted by states all across the country, then the kids who don't choose college are not having their needs met. A student who plans to become an electrician, for example, does not need a college-prep curriculum.

Standardized tests are a relatively cheap and easy way to categorize students, but the multiple choice format pretty much narrows learning to memorization of subject matter. And unfortunately, if absolutely everything hinges on high stakes tests, then the test is what will be taught.

Yet, teaching to a test turns students into passive receivers of knowledge rather than active participants in the learning process. Facts taught out of context are not retained, and test drill kills inquiry, curiosity, and creativity.

Educators believe that the purpose of education is to teach students to think. A student who can think critically uses mental processes of discernment, analysis, and evaluation to make decisions and draw conclusions.

Understanding how to learn serves all students, no matter what they plan to do in life. The electrician who troubleshoots your electrical system doesn't need a bachelor's degree, but she does need to be able to problem solve.

Educators know that a test—any test—is but one quick stop on a student's learning journey. If he's been taught how to learn, it is a journey of discovery.

It's simple: If you teach a child to pass a test, he will learn for a day. If you teach a child to understand how he learns, he will learn for a lifetime.

Educators don't want to prepare students to take tests. They know that there is more to learning than subject matter, and that human beings play more roles than that of worker.

So before we move forward in education reform we need to decide: Are we educating students for a test?

Or for a lifetime?

QUIRKY BRILLIANCE AND BUBBLE TESTS

Think for a minute about the smartest people you know. Just what makes them so smart?

Perhaps the smartest person you know is the one who is completely versed and up-to-date on politics or current events. Or maybe it's the one whose head holds the most trivia, the friend you'd phone if you were a contestant on *Who Wants To Be a Millionaire?*

Maybe it's the person who, without any real training, can take apart your broken toaster and put it back together again. What about the person who is highly mechanical, but is not very good at reading people, the one who wouldn't know intuition if it knocked on the door and announced its arrival? Is she more or less intelligent than a highly intuitive person?

And how about a photographic memory? Does that make a person smart? Or just lucky?

Everyone knows people whose intelligence is not well-balanced, for example, those individuals who are terrible at math, but are fast readers with extensive vocabularies. Which smarts count for more there?

We all know people who are book smart but can't seem to get their lives organized. And we also know people without a lick of higher education who manage to make successful, happy lives for themselves.

And how about those philosophical types, the ones who spend their lives contemplating the big picture? Are they the smartest of us all?

The truth is, we all have varying degrees of many kinds of intelligence. And it's the quirky combinations that make us interesting. Life would be a snooze if we were all the same.

Sadly, federal and state governments across this country believe that children are only as smart as their test scores. And once students take those tests and are slapped with that label, they are sorted: Successful. Unsuccessful.

The student becomes the score. It goes into their permanent record and supposedly tells us everything we need to know about them as learners. Then those scores are compiled and used to give their school a score. Then they're used to give their teachers a score.

To what extent that number will impact a child's life is hard to say. On one hand, it might spur them—and their parents—to take a more active role in schoolwork. On the other hand, it might simply make a child feel stupid and inadequate.

The truth is, no standardized test can measure or describe the rich, complex mix of gifts and talent that are your child. And yet, there's a lot at stake when your child sits down with that Number 2 pencil and starts bubbling—a lot at stake for your child's teacher and school, anyway.

Whether that single score is going to make a significant difference in your child's life is anyone's guess.

OUT OF STEP BUT STILL MOVING

Is your child smart?

How smart? When you listen to him play with his friends, does he figure things out as quickly as they do? Or does it take him a bit longer?

If you acknowledged secretly to yourself that maybe your child is not quite as quick as his friends, not slow mind you, just not the quickest, how does it make you feel?

Do you love him any less? Are you embarrassed by him?

Of course not.

Because you value other qualities, too, like honesty and kindness. And besides, you know intelligence takes many forms. He might struggle with schoolwork, but he can fix your broken weed whacker. He might not be a fast reader, but he can rattle off the batting average of every player in the Boston Red Sox and name every leading scorer in the NBA. You know that he's learning, he just needs to go about it his own way, at his own pace.

That's how most parents feel. Sure, it might be nice to have a baby Einstein, but you don't love them any less if they're not. Above all, parents want their kids to know how to learn, and to feel good about themselves as learners.

And yet, education policy makers in the United States do not recognize the not-so-fast learner. In fact, under current education legislation, his school will be punished if he does not learn as much, as fast, as the U.S. Department of Education says he should.

That's the absurdity of current education reform. It lures you in with noble-sounding rhetoric—No Child Left Behind, Race to the Top—and then dons the gloves, delivering a one-two punch to school districts whose clientele don't, for both obvious and elusive reasons, achieve at the same rate.

But because children all start at different places and move forward at different rates, the best way to measure their progress is to use a growth model, which tracks a student's individual achievement from one year to the next. So if a child starts sixth grade reading at a third grade level, but he ends the year reading at a fifth grade level, he has made tremendous progress. He may not be at grade level yet, but in this school year he has moved up two grade levels.

Current education reform revolves around the standardized test. Every student must achieve the same amount, at the same rate. Current education reform does not acknowledge that having less ability, or different ability, affects the level of achievement. It does not acknowledge that some students may achieve less, or achieve more slowly, but may still achieve their personal best. A growth model would acknowledge that.

And that's what should count.

Educators get this. Most parents get it, too.

Unfortunately, the Department of Education doesn't. And that's the saddest absurdity of all.

RIGOR AND RELEVANCE MEAN SQUAT WITHOUT THE RELATIONSHIP

Rigor. Relevance. Relationships.

These three Rs are the latest, greatest magic elixir that will supposedly transform education as we know it.

The theory behind this educational trend is that if we raise the level of our expectations and make the work rigorous, choose educational experiences that are relevant, and concentrate on creating good relationships, all children will learn. It's got a good ring to it, which is why it's been bandied about so much and is hailed as the new three Rs of learning.

But the dirty truth is that rigor has squeezed out both relevance and relationships.

All over the country states have mandated more rigor, many now requiring that every high school student, college bound or not, pursue a college prep curriculum. Yet the new requirements so completely fill a student's schedule that it leaves little room for electives—which are often of most relevance to students. Teaching to the almighty standardized test is rigorous, too, though it's questionable whether or not those tests are relevant.

Students tell us that much of what they're forced to study is irrelevant. That doesn't mean that it is, just that they perceive it that way. Students repeatedly say that they want hands-on lessons, learning that is immediately useful.

But creating more meaningful relationships in education? We're doing nothing more than paying lip service to that. In today's test-driven, data-dominated, documentation-crazed, super-consolidated world of education, the relationship is the first thing to go. We're so busy processing students that we lose sight of the real live human beings behind the numbers and stats. There's almost no time in the school day for getting to know each other.

Guiding and nurturing young people into becoming productive adults, and the joy of connecting with kids, is why teachers teach. And students crave teachers who take the time to care about them as a person and recognize their individuality. But adding rigor for the student adds it for the teacher, too, which would be fine if it didn't squeeze out relationship-building time with kids.

Experts point to that disconnect, that lack of relationships with positive adult role models, as one reason for so much school violence. Too many kids are just plain lonely. They can't always verbalize it, but they crave connections with people who care about them and who celebrate their individuality.

Here's the thing that noneducators just don't get: the relationship is the key to both rigor and relevance. A student will work hard for a teacher that "gets" them, a teacher that they like and respect. And they'll really listen when that teacher explains the relevance of what they're doing.

Rigor? Bring it on.

Relevance? Absolutely.

But without a relationship to build on? It's just more educational rhetoric.

A MOST IMPORTANT MISSION

"Ms. Thayer, I just can't make up my mind. So when I grow up I'm going to be a pediatrician, but I'll do hair at a salon in my spare time."

So says an eighth grade girl during a career project. She has a 1.5 grade point average and scores two grades below average in reading comprehension. Most of the boys are certain—unequivocally—that they will become professional athletes, including the scrawny ones who play on no athletic team whatsoever.

Ms. Thayer is torn. Should she burst the bubble and point these kids in a more realistic direction? Or should she play the consummate cheerleader and encourage them to follow their dreams no matter what?

Public schools try to do too much. But one thing they don't do enough of is career education. Bullied by legislators who dictate the Priority-of-the-Year, too often schools have little time or money to spend on career exploration.

Yet, what is school if not a place to prepare for the future? If public schools don't do it, who will? Where else can kids learn about career options? Television? They'll end up thinking that being a lawyer is like *L. A. Law*, all courtroom drama, but no paperwork. That being a surgeon is like *Grey's Anatomy*, all sex in the supply closet and no hard work.

You get out of education what you put into it, and parents can do a lot to supplement their child's education no matter what school they attend. But this is one area where most parents need help. Chances are, their own career experience has been pretty limited, too.

Public schools need to do more than tell kids what subjects they test well in. They need to get more hands-on experiences into kids' hands.

Ms. Thayer's school has a beautiful career center that too often sits empty. Student schedules are so full that they have little time to spend there. And truthfully, many kids just aren't motivated enough to spend their spare time researching careers if it's not required.

A few fortunate kids start college knowing exactly what they want to be when they grow up. But most don't. Many students admit they're biding their time in college, worrying about the day they'll have to declare a major. Some change majors, which is costly and time-consuming. Some go on to graduate school simply because they don't know what to do next.

If there were more time in a student's schedule for career exploration, from grade school on up, school would seem more relevant to kids. And if school were more relevant, maybe grade point averages and test scores would go up, too.

Schools teach kids the skills they need to join the work force. But they're so busy testing them on those skills that they ignore where they'll apply them when they graduate.

In the short run, a rich, thriving career program will result in focused students who are more engaged in their education. In the long run, it will result in adults who find careers that they love.

YOU GOTTA HAVE ART

When money gets tight education reform that suggests a no-nonsense, no-frills approach makes a lot of sense to a lot of people. Reading and math, they reason, are more important than finger painting and sing-a-longs.

But wait. Right this minute, stop and think of a piece of music that speaks to your soul, something that takes you to another time and place. Is it a honky-tonk with Garth Brooks? A nightclub with Dean Martin? A symphony hall with Ludwig van Beethoven? Did it take you to a time in your life that was happy? Or sad?

Now imagine if this music had not been written. What if the artist had been forced to take another science class at the expense of his music career? What if she'd never sat down at the piano or been handed a guitar?

What a dull, flat, colorless world this would be. Without the arts, all of the things that thrill us, the music we turn to for solace or joy, the movies we love, the art that warms our homes, the very expression of our culture, will suffer.

Without the arts there is no *life*, to life.

Sure, widgets are important. And sure, big business believes we should build them faster, better, and more cheaply. But should we sacrifice one for the other? And if we can build a better widget, shouldn't we be able to come up with a way to keep the arts in schools?

What students get from the arts can't be reliably or concretely measured. And that's why the arts are the first to go when money gets tight, and why they're being cut, right now, in schools everywhere to focus on high stakes testing.

What education reformers forget is that we are put on this earth to fulfill our own individual destinies, to become our true selves, to reach our highest potential. That's not going to look the same for all kids.

For some the destiny is science, technology, engineering, and math. But not for all.

Some kids will be absolutely miserable if forced into a curriculum that does not suit them. For some, a school without the arts is a place to avoid.

We can't leave those kids out. They deserve to have their needs met as surely as does the future engineer.

And if we give artistic kids what they need to thrive, we are ultimately giving to ourselves as well.

IMAGE MAKER, IMAGE BREAKER

Ms. Mitchell's cleavage was the cause of the commotion.

Not because she was well-endowed. She wasn't. And her stretchy top and khaki pants looked crisp and neat. But something about the combination of that apricot-colored scoop neck, peaches and cream complexion, long legs, and thick shiny hair made that twenty-three-year-old body look so ripe every freshman boy's mouth watered.

Fifty-five-year-old Ms. Owens wears stretchy scoop necks, too. But three inches of deep cleavage on a size eighteen doesn't result in neck-wrenching double-takes by teen-age boys. More pillowy than perky, her chest just looks like a nice place to nap.

When it is suggested by her principal that she not wear scoop neck tops any more, Ms. Mitchell takes issue. Did he have the same talk with Ms. Owens?

On Friday, a day when casual dress is permitted, first-year teacher Mr. Franzen comes to school in a sharp-looking maize and blue athletic suit, emblazoned with the logo of his alma mater, and expensive, spotless white tennies. Only on Fridays does he feel completely and utterly himself.

Down the hall, Mr. Baldacci, who is not a supporter of "casual day," wears a wrinkled white dress shirt and a plaid tie, four and a half inches wide and knotted in a double Windsor. His pants are from the seventies, too, of a polyester so sturdy they'll be unearthed and studied by anthropologists in the next millennium. He's had the same black dress shoes for twenty years and as long as he keeps the scuffs covered with polish and replaces the Dr. Scholl's inserts regularly, he figures they'll last until he retires.

Why doesn't that man buy some decent clothes? Mr. Franzen wonders when Mr. Baldacci passes by, wrinkled shirt coming un-tucked, ancient leather belt straining at the last hole.

Mr. Baldacci nods cordially to Mr. Franzen, but shakes his head once he is past. *An athletic suit to school? Are you kidding me?*

So, just exactly how casual is too casual for teacher dress in school?

It's an issue districts across the country struggle with as their workforce becomes younger. And it's sometimes a point of contention between new and veteran teachers.

Buttoned up teachers are annoyed by sloppy colleagues and immodest rookies. They say the rubber flip-flops, short shorts, and college logo sweats should be left at home.

Those dressed more casually, however, wish the old school would lighten up. Fresh-from-college teachers want their students to relate to them. Their image, they believe, is closely tied to the way they dress. And let's face it; there may be something to the idea that it's easier to connect with kids if you look fun and approachable. But there also may be something to the idea that a teacher in a suit or tie projects a more authoritative presence to students.

Most districts have some sort of dress code for teachers, but often the terminology is vague. "Dress professionally" leaves room for interpretation. This perplexes administrators who sometimes choose to simply look the other way until a parent complains. And because teachers are master rule setters themselves, they're quick to find loopholes in someone else's rules.

In all fairness, many workplaces have become more casual. "Business casual" in some places is now considered to be professional dress, and jeans have become "business casual." Rumpled dot com tycoons have changed the way we look at success.

And though teachers young and old have definite ideas about teacher appearance, they do agree that as professionals they should not be told how to dress.

And then there's that other problem with judging someone's attire: it's not only what you wear, but also how you wear it. Is a wrinkled shirt and tie better than neatly pressed dark blue jeans? Can a less endowed woman get away with a lower-cut top than a busty one?

The strange dichotomy is that while teachers rarely notice what their students are wearing, students often notice—and make fun of—every detail of their teacher's clothing, right down to a missing button.

So, do clothes make the man? Or the woman?

Is a better-dressed teacher a better teacher?

How much does teacher dress reflect respect for the education process?

And if we could just get over it all, would we be better off?

Yes, we want to teach kids that certain jobs come with particular responsibilities, including dress requirements. We also want to teach them not to judge a book by its cover.

Ultimately, the most important question is, if teachers dressed like really important people, would they finally be treated as such?

GOLDIE'S JOY

Ms. Blume's fourth hour students burst through the door each day, bouncing off the walls with caffeine and lunchtime drama. Once they settled down they were a really great class. It just took so darned long to settle them.

"Okay," she sing-songed, clapping her hands to get their attention. "Let's all take a deep breath...and let it out sloooowly...and have a moment of quiet...quiet...quiet..." she lowered her voice with each word. "...and get ready to learn."

This fleeting meditative moment was not part of a specific program. It was simply Ms. Blume's instinctual need for self-preservation. By calming the students she calmed herself and the lesson went much more smoothly.

As it turns out, her instincts were right. Actress Goldie Hawn, founder of The Hawn Foundation, promotes the benefits of mindfulness in the classroom. The program is called MindUP and it is a curriculum rooted in neuroscience. It provides detailed lessons to teach children strategies to cultivate concentration skills, observation, and relaxation to increase clarity and center their attention.

The world moves fast for children. They're bombarded with an enormous amount of flashing, blinking, noisy stimuli through television, DVDs, iPods, smartphones, and animated toys. They're over-exposed to conflict, aggression, and violence. This takes its toll in the classroom, resulting in short attention spans and anger issues. But by teaching simple mindfulness techniques, students can learn to reduce their own anxiety and stress and heighten their readiness for academic performance.

Imagine how that would look in the classroom: children with the skills to shake off excess stimuli and focus on their school work, children with the skills to calm themselves and make good choices, children who feel connected to (and compassionate toward) others, children who are confident and optimistic, who feel joy instead of fear.

The change would be profound.

Though it might sound like something from the mod, mod world, it really isn't. It's simply a common-sense approach to improving learning.

And the benefits are far-reaching. Not only do calm kids learn better, but they get along better, too. That means that discipline issues, which take a huge toll on learning, improve as well.

Education reformers spend so much time arguing about what students should learn and how they should be tested on it, that they completely ignore whether or not students are in the right frame of mind to learn. This approach is refreshing because it considers the whole child, not simply his test score. It's exciting to imagine the impact such a concept might have on learning.

So, can something this simple trump the highly politicized, corporate driven education reform that we are witnessing today?

You bet your sweet bippy.

THE PETER PRINCIPLE, ALIVE AND WELL

The ladder is narrow and short for people looking to move up in education. There aren't many top jobs in each district, and there are only about three rungs above the position of teacher.

So if the goal is to make a lot of money by becoming an education leader, job-hopping is required. If a superintendent stays in one district the pay increases will be relatively small. But a move to a different, larger district can bring big money.

And that's okay. Everyone has the right to pursue the highest salary they can. But it means that superintendent turnover is huge, and everyone seems to know it except the school boards that do the hiring. They continue to hire outsiders, believing that they'll stay forever, while ignoring excellent candidates within their own ranks.

When a superintendent hops from district to district, never staying longer than two years, his ability is as illusory as the Wizard's. He sells a flashy idea, but never has to prove that it works. As soon as he leaves another superintendent comes along selling a different flashy idea, creating a different illusion. A superintendent who knows he is not going to stay can say absolutely anything he wants to about what he knows and can do. He will be long gone before he has to prove it.

Ultimately, the people who are left behind, students, parents, educators, and community, pay the price. They're left with low morale, hodgepodge programs, and an undone to-do list.

A wise school board chooses someone with strong roots in their own community, someone who will have to answer to friends and family, someone who understands the district's history, culture, and traditions. Someone who will stay around to see if the changes work.

To make matters worse, school boards often pay big bucks for superintendent searches by companies that know nothing about the district, its clientele, and its needs. To Mr. DeMille, that concept seems silly. His district spent thousands of public tax dollars to find a "perfect fit."

Representatives from the company set up shop in the teachers' lounge for a few days, chatting with staff and passing out surveys. Munching his tuna on rye, Mr. DeMille watched from across the room as the search company interviewed staff members about what they wanted in a superintendent. He kept thinking about the fact that these people were strangers from out of state, not at all familiar with the culture of his beloved district.

To him, it just didn't add up; why pay strangers big money to do something Human Resources could do? Wasn't that the purpose of Human Resources anyway? How could the people in this company possibly know them better than they knew themselves?

Mr. DeMille pondered this as he sat in the lounge listening to the friendly lady question his colleagues. Finally, he piped up.

"What, exactly, do you do for the $10,000 our district is paying you?" he asked.

The nice lady smiled.

"We survey the staff and community to find out what they want in a superintendent," she said. "Then we find candidates who match that description."

"Well, where do you find them?" Mr. DeMille asked.

"From education agencies and web searches," the smiling lady said.

"Well what, exactly, do you do that we couldn't do ourselves?" he asked. "I mean, we can survey our own staff and community. We can find candidates in journals and newspapers."

Apparently, Mr. DeMille went too far. The smiling lady stopped smiling. But he couldn't stop.

"It just seems like a lot of money to pay for something we could do ourselves," he persisted.

The nice lady packed up in a huff and marched off to another lounge.

Mr. DeMille thought about that conversation a lot over the next few years as he watched the superintendent they eventually hired alienate staff, dismantle their school culture and traditions, promote top-down management over site-based decision making, destroy staff morale, and basically tick off just about everyone she came in contact with.

He didn't know if she grew as tired of them as they did of her, if she was forced out, or if it was just time for a career move but eventually, that superintendent started looking elsewhere.

And guess what?

Soon she was one of the top three candidates for a big district out of state, and then there was an interview team from that district in the lounge, this time asking all kinds of questions about her performance.

What a dilemma. If they told the truth and the superintendent didn't get the job, they could be stuck with her forever. But if they were crafty, they just might be rid of her. This may be their only chance! What to do, *what to do?*

Well. They did the only thing they could do.

They gave her a glowing report.

MERIT PAY WON'T SOLVE ANYTHING

Slackers.

The word is unspoken but implied every time policy makers discuss merit pay for teachers. It reflects the bizarre but persistent notion that there is one right, effective way to teach, and most teachers are too lazy to do it.

And the truth is, just like in every other profession, there are a few slackers. Not a lot, mind you, and certainly not hoards as the media would have you believe. But a few.

Like Mr. Williams. Consummate lounge lizard, Mr. Williams lets a student keep attendance, never gives homework, and his lesson plan consists of a workbook. It's hard to imagine what his evaluations look like, but based on the amount of time he spends kissing up, they're probably glowing.

Ms. Lansens, on the other hand, works her behind off. And it ticks her off royally to see Slacker Man spend hours drinking coffee and chatting up the secretaries while she slogs through another stack of student essays, or comes in at 6 a.m. to set up for a big project.

Ninety-nine percent of her colleagues are hard working, dedicated people who perform small miracles every day. But there's waste in every profession: careless doctors, incompetent lawyers, dishonest CEOs, lazy line workers.

Tying teacher pay to student test scores won't change that.

If Ms. Lansens' pay is based on how she stacked up next to the slacker, she'd be in like Flynn. But if her pay is based on the test scores of her students? Some years she'd be eating steak and lobster because the learning happens so effortlessly. The year she taught Reading and Writing Lab, on the other hand, it would have been nothing but weenies and beans. The nineteen special education students in that class made every lesson a battle of wills.

Noneducators think teachers should be held accountable. Good teachers agree. Most would love to be recognized for good attendance, innovative lesson plans, committee involvement, professional development, ability to work with staff and community.

But they don't want to be held accountable for things that are out of their control, like student attendance, low IQ, poor parenting, and yes, low test scores. Too many variables contribute to those scores.

And consider this: Countless teachers make huge impacts in troubled students' lives, even if they aren't able to raise their test scores. They teach them social skills, manners, hygiene, sportsmanship, fair play and the difference between right and wrong. They teach basic life skills to students who sometimes start from so far behind, they have a long way to travel to catch up. Teachers feed them, clothe them, and play mom and dad to them.

Does that have less merit?

And if grades are inflated now, just wait. Teachers are pressured every day by parents and administrators to raise grades. Imagine if their salary depends on it, too.

As a solution to what ails education, merit pay for teachers is shortsighted and narrow. The problems are rooted in society, not the teaching staff.

Still, merit pay is worth looking into. And since it's their bright idea, let's start with politicians. No perks, no pay raises until they prove their worth.

What? That's not fair? We can't hold politicians accountable for the woes of the constituents they represent?

Really.

Up On Capitol Hilltop
(Sung to the tune of "Up on the Rooftop")

Up on the hilltop
Pols pass laws,
They act as if they're Santa Claus.
"Fixing" education
Is their gift
But true learning issues
Get short shrift.

Ho, ho, ho!
Government's the foe!
Go, go, go!
Public schools to overthrow!
Up on the hilltop,
Slick, slick, slick,
Just one more
Political gimmick.

First comes the NAEP test
For little Nell,
Joy of learning
Gets death knell
Give her a voucher
If her school fails
Make her education
Go retail.

Ho, ho, ho!
Testing woe!
Ho, ho, ho!
Another low blow!
Up on the hilltop,
Another dirty trick,
They have the answer;
Political shtick.

While your school crumbles

They pass NCLB
Then go on a
Spending spree
There's nothing left
For your funding needs
Down go schools in
Bankruptcy.

Low, low, low!
Tight politico!
Owe, owe, owe!
Funding no show!
Up on the hilltop
They live high
Money for schools
In short supply.

Whether an elephant
Or an ass
Corporate says "jump"
And a law they'll pass
They won't rest
'til they privatize it all
True progress
They will stonewall.

Ho, ho, ho!
Quid pro quo!
Ho, ho, ho!
Follow the dough!
Up on the hilltop,
They bootlick
Down thru' the ages
Fool the public.

Pols need facts
to fit their goals
Put their "experts"
On the payroll
Lobbyists with kickbacks
Have last word
While educators
Go unheard.

No, no, no!
Don't ask the pros
Whoa, whoa, whoa!
The "trenches" don't know

Up on the hilltop
It's political gain
Public education
Down the drain!

ORDINARY PEOPLE, EXTRAORDINARY HEART

Okay, so all teachers aren't perfect.

In fact, a lot of them are just plain ordinary. Competent, yes. But fairly average, too.

What can be done about that, though? A look around most any workplace reveals only a few truly extraordinary employees.

The highly qualified requirements of the No Child Left Behind Act address a teacher's knowledge of subject. But a teacher can know their subject backward and forward and still be a "bad" teacher.

Think for a moment about the teachers you didn't like. It had nothing to do with how well they knew their material, did it? In fact, most teachers do know their material. That's the easy part of being a teacher. The hard part is far less tangible. The hard part is being inspiring, and connecting with kids every minute of every day.

The "bad" teachers are the ones who antagonize kids. They're mean-spirited and impatient and indifferent. The "bad" teachers have unimaginative lesson plans. They think that being right is more important than being kind. They're lazy and disorganized and unwilling to try something new.

But the best teachers? The best teachers are firm, but warm. Inspiring and creative. Organized, yet flexible. They're funny and fun and quick to laugh—even at themselves.

You can't legislate that.

That's why the highly qualified legislation in NCLB misses the mark. It boils good teaching down to credentials on paper.

Teacher bashers have a lot to say about teacher quality. When they complain about public schools in general and teachers specifically, one has to wonder, "Okay, so what's the solution? Fire them all? Then what? Where can be found enough teachers, let alone enough extraordinary teachers, to fill those positions?"

The human pool is mostly filled with pretty average people.

If they fired every teacher today and replaced them, the new teachers would face exactly the same problems in the classroom. They're just ordinary people, too.

We've all had a few extraordinary teachers in our lifetimes. But only a few. Yet we want our children's teachers to be all extraordinary, all the time.

It's a lovely idea.

But how realistic is it?

If the profession was more respected, and the job included more parental and administrative support, and if the salaries were higher, would that draw the best and the brightest to the classroom and ensure that all teachers were extraordinary all the time?

One thing is certain: teacher bashing doesn't work. Disdain and antagonism toward teachers just makes them defensive. And if they're busy being defensive, they aren't at their best.

That's the problem with just about every facet of education reform. It's more about blame than support.

According to the *MetLife Survey of the American Teacher, Teachers, Parents and the Economy,* March 2012, "Teacher job satisfaction has dropped 15 points since 2009, from 59% who were very satisfied to 44% who are very satisfied, the lowest level in over 20 years. The percentage of teachers who say they are very or fairly likely to leave the profession has increased by 12 points since 2009, from 17% to 29%."

So instead of passing legislation that does nothing except serve politicians and corporations, we need education reform that gets to the heart of good teaching.

Because that's what good teaching is—all heart.

STOP TELLING ME WHAT I NEED (AND DON'T GIVE ME WHAT YOU NEED)

Riiiing!

"Hello, Ms. Rawlings, fifth grade teacher speaking."

"*Hel-lo*, this is Glen Gladhander, your state legislator, and boy, have I got good news for you! We've got $39 million in our state budget agreement that will revolutionize education. In fact, it's going to make you a more effective teacher and bring your students full speed into the age of technology."

"Wow! Really? Does that mean I'm finally getting—"

"Yes, ma'am, are you ready for this?! We're going to give every fifth grader in the state a laptop computer!"

"Ah. I see. A laptop. Every fifth grader. Wow. Well, thank you. That's very generous of you. I assume you surveyed teachers to see what they—"

"Generous is my middle name! Nothing's too good for education in my state! By October every child in your class will have a shiny new laptop! In fact, in six years every single student will have a laptop, too!"

"Sounds wonderful. Who, exactly, is responsible for them? Can the kids take them home?"

"Home, church, vacation, you name it!"

"So the kids will have to tote them around. . .their bookbags are full and heavy as it is. . . hmmm. . . If they don't take them home, where, exactly, will

I keep them? My classroom's small, and my one cabinet that locks isn't big enough to hold thirty laptops. . ."

"Well, hon, you might just have to get yourself some new cabinets."

". . . and you know, just because each child has a laptop doesn't mean they'll have Internet access at home."

"Then they'll hook 'em up in your classroom."

"Great! So they'll be putting Internet access in my classroom? Can my district afford that? And what about electricity? Our tech people keep telling us that our building is old and the wiring isn't equipped to handle so many computers. Will they rewire the whole building? And will the laptops be networked?"

"Networks? Ah. . .maybe CNN. . "

"Hmmm. . .I see. Well, kids lose stuff all the time. What happens when they lose it? It's not exactly like losing a textbook, you know. I won't be able to just hand them another one. If we're doing a lesson on the laptop, what about the kids who forgot it at home?"

"Well, uh—"

". . . and what about theft? What happens when Johnny gets his laptop stolen?"

"Well, uh—"

". . . and what about repairs? Kids are hard on equipment. Did you allocate money for maintenance and repairs? And what about kids who break them repeatedly? What do they do while their laptop is being repaired?"

"Well, little lady, you're a smart girl, I'm sure you'll figure that out."

". . . and what about printers? Will we get printers, too? They'll need to print their work. And what about ink cartridges? A class of thirty will go through cartridges pretty fast and ink is *so* expensive. . .oh, and viruses, will they have good virus protection?"

"Well, uh—"

". . . and what about upgrades? In a few years, the laptops this first class gets will be outdated. Then what?"

"Well, we'll just cross that bridge when we come to it. Don't you worry about that now, you let me worry about that!"

". . . and when will I be trained on how to integrate the laptop into my curriculum? I mean, summer's almost over so it's too late to do it now. And once school starts there's so little time for intensive training. How will I. . .?"

"Curricu-what?"

"The curriculum. It's so full already there's no room to add anything extra. I have to work the laptops into what we're already covering. . ."

"Like I said, you're a real smart cookie. Why, with all the education you got, you'll figure that out in a snap!"

"Riiight. Will the laptops be equipped with programs that fit into my curriculum? Will they help me meet the state standards and benchmarks? I mean, the kids will just play on Facebook and fill them up with games if you let them. It could end up being a very expensive game toy."

"Stands, benches, games? We talkin' stadiums here? How 'bout Detroit's Comerica Park—!"

"I'm sorry, sir, I certainly don't mean to seem ungrateful, but there are a lot of things that. . ."

"Okay, missy, gotta run. I got a meeting with some guys from IBM, then lunch with Tigers Owner Mike Ilitch. Tigers have finally improved since we built them that new stadium. Maybe we can free up a few dollars for the Lions. . ."

STEP UP TO THE PLATE AND EVALUATE

When the principal walked in, Mr. Harbach assumed he'd come to talk about a student. When the principal sat down at a desk with pen and clipboard, to which an evaluation form was attached, he couldn't believe his eyes.

It was the very last day of school in June.

He wasn't formally evaluated again until eight years later.

He didn't complain. For a perfectionist, evaluations are always nerve-racking, sweat-generating, panic-producing experiences. He was happy to slide under the radar.

Mr. Harbach likes to think that so much time passed between evaluations because he is such a top-notch teacher. He's sure his superiors know he has things under control from casual observation, or from passing by his open classroom door. They don't need to be in his classroom to know that he handles all of his own discipline, keeps good records and turns his grades in on time. Perhaps they hear good things from his students and their parents, too.

After all, any good administrator has her finger on the pulse of the building and knows the strengths and weaknesses of her staff. And besides, Mr. Harbach remembers that second year teacher, Ms. Romulus, who didn't cut it and got evaluated right out of a job, so he knows they're evaluating some, if not him.

So he is surprised when he hears an acquaintance at his son's soccer game grumble, "Oh, those unions. Once those bad teachers get tenure they can never be fired."

That persistent yet false assumption is not true. Tenure is not a job guarantee. Tenure laws clearly outline procedures that allow school administrators to fire incompetent teachers, whether they have tenure or not.

Too often, though, where the system breaks down is in the evaluation process. Evaluations take time. Documentation is required. But money shortfalls mean administrative staffs get cut and remaining administrators are spread too thin. When time is tight, time-consuming teacher evaluations might fall to the bottom of the list. Which is probably what happened with Mr. Harbach's last-day-of-school evaluation. The busy principal forgot, then rushed to do it at the last minute to meet a quota.

And too, people who work in schools tend to be...well...nice. They're caretakers. They don't want to hurt anyone's feelings. Administrators may be reluctant to use the evaluation process on a senior teacher who is an old friend, someone with whom they came up through the ranks. So maybe they look the other way and hope that teacher retires soon.

The teachers on Mr. Harbach's staff certainly know who the "bad" teacher is, and they want her gone. She reflects badly on all of them. In the lounge there is much whispered speculation about why administrators don't get tough and just evaluate her out of the system.

Rather than tackle the sticky issue of evaluations with teachers close to retirement, many administrators have chosen to concentrate on the new crop of teachers coming in. Determined not to make any hiring mistakes, they've beefed up the evaluation process and immediately terminate the ones who don't show promise. It's also important to note that when done well, the evaluation process can help a so-so teacher improve.

That's the thing, though; the process is only as good as the people who use it.

ALL THERE FOR THE TAKING

Drop-out rates, low test scores, too many Es, teacher quality, merit pay, tenure, professional development, Common Core Standards, Gates-funded teacher evaluations, charter schools, vouchers, scripted lessons, differentiated instruction, extended school years, and most strenuously, standardized testing.

What can be done to improve education? According to legislators and corporate reformers, the list is endless.

But that list leaves out one very important piece of the puzzle.

The responsibility of the student.

See, what everyone seems to forget is that it's all there for the taking. If someone wants an education in this country they can have it, tuition free. Teachers, materials, information, textbooks, workbooks, journals, reference books, videos, technology and lab equipment are available, to one degree or another, in every single school.

And what's more, almost every school offers more than academics. Art rooms are filled with paints and paper, music rooms with pianos and sheet music, theaters with playbooks and props, and in many cases vocational classes introduce students to careers such as healthcare or building trades.

Even the poorest schools are full of information and people who are ready, willing, and able—aching, actually—to teach a student who wants to learn. It makes teachers nearly weep with frustration to see bright, capable, talented children slide lazily along, refusing to take part in the bounty of knowledge that is offered to them.

All any student has to do is open the books, read the material, study for the quiz, write the paper, listen to the teacher, and *try.*

The steady drumbeat spewed by corporate reformers continuously, relentlessly, incorrectly, and nauseatingly bashes the public school system in America, as if they are solely to blame for low test scores.

They're not.

Children in this country have been sold a bill of goods that says they are responsible for nothing, it is our duty to spoon feed them, if they don't like the system we'll change it, if they screw up we'll cover for them, everything will be handed to them, and it's all their teachers' fault.

Whether it's an allowance or a grade, kids need to know that they have to work for what they want.

Education reformers rant that the public school system needs to "improve outcomes." Well, how about improving input? How about parents sending us students who are eager to learn so that we don't have to force-feed them?

It's time to tell the kids in this country: get your butts to school, sit down, be quiet, do your work, quit whining, and make your parents proud.

THE BOTTOM LINE

Walk down the halls of a high school on any given day and peek into the classrooms. The single-minded dedication of teachers as they present material to students can, on a good day, be positively awe inspiring.

The door of each classroom frames a snapshot: Kids with heads bent over microscopes studying amoebas. Kids crowded around the physics teacher as he demonstrates a law of motion. Kids giggling as they stumble over the words of Shakespeare. Kids' faces tight with concentration as they work out quadratic equations in geometry.

There's a magical feeling in a high school when classes are in session, teachers are teaching, and students are learning. The school sort of thrums and pulses with a low-level hum, a quiet buzz.

It feels holy. Sacred. Divine.

But it's not the school itself. It's not the teachers. It's not even the students that create the buzz. The buzz is what happens when the three come together.

The buzz is the Pursuit of Knowledge.

And that's where every piece of education legislation goes astray—by revering the outcome rather than the pursuit.

It's time to change that. It's time to resolve to hold the Pursuit of Knowledge as a sacred trust, to resolve to approach the *pursuit* with the same reverence one would show to a sacrament.

For it is the *pursuit* that is the deity. Not the test scores. Not the grade point average. Not the rating by Standard & Poor's. It's the pursuit itself, the effort, the endeavor, the *attempt to learn* that should be venerated.

All learning is valuable, but the learning that takes place in the primary and secondary school settings is especially sacrosanct, because the students are all initiates. They're here because they have to be, not by choice. These first experiences will shape how they approach the pursuit of knowledge for the rest of their lives.

And because what they experience here will determine how they feel about learning for the rest of their lives, every single detail of their experience here should be executed with the utmost care and treated with reverence.

It's almost a given that people will go out of their way to help a pregnant woman or a child in need. It's an unspoken understanding that for the most part, society protects the vulnerable. So it should be for schools and those in them, from the superintendent to the custodian, because they are all part of a grand, magnificent ceremony.

It should be the collective effort of every person to place the education of our youth at the very top of the priority list because that is the key to success for our society, our planet, our future.

Until every person in every community makes it their business to treat the educational system with reverence, education won't be "fixed."

Imagine a world where people bow their heads in reverence upon entering a school.

Imagine a world where people genuflect toward the textbooks that hold the information that will teach our children to read and write.

Imagine a world where people give freely to schools when the collection plate is passed.

Once the *pursuit* of knowledge is considered to be sacred, the rest will fall into place.

Amen.

Conclusion

It's noon, the very best part of my teaching day. My fifth hour students burst through the door, drop heavy backpacks on desks, and talk all at once, chattering excitedly about today's agenda.

The truth is, though, that there is not one agenda here. This is the Advanced Journalism-Newspaper class, and though we are all working together toward one common goal—the publication of our award-winning student newspaper—the fact is that each of the twenty-six students in this class is working on something different. That means, in essence, that I create twenty-six different lesson plans for this class each day.

But I don't care. I love it. I have never worked so hard in my life as I do on this class. Neither have most of the students in it. For us, this class is the icing on the cake, the cherry on the sundae, the shiny gold star at the top of the paper.

We look forward to this hour all day long.

Kim and Sarah get busy on layout, struggling to fit a ten-inch story into a nine-inch space. Matt is using Adobe Photoshop to design an infographic, a skill he has worked hard to perfect. Brandon is writing his column, a witty and wry commentary on sports, politics, and the life of a teen. Brynn is preparing invoices to mail to the businesses that advertise in our paper. Rob is uploading photos he took with the digital camera, conferring with Kim and Sarah about which ones to use in the layout. Kirstie taps her pencil against her desk, deep in thought, trying to come up with a provocative, clever headline for Matt's infographic. Melodee does the final tweak on a breathtakingly sensitive article about a student with HIV.

In addition to their individual areas of interest, each student will write at least one article per issue, either news, feature, opinion, or sports. Each will also sell advertising space to businesses to generate the money necessary to print 2,500 copies of this sixteen-page paper each month.

Students work on various tasks while they wait their turn to talk with me about their articles; we'll discuss whom they should interview, how to get in touch with those people, and possible angles to take with the story. At the computers several students work quietly on second drafts, correcting the errors marked by my dreaded red pen.

I will have most of these kids in class for four years straight. Typically, they take my Beginning Journalism class as freshmen, and then take Advanced Journalism as many years as they can fit it into their schedule.

The changes I witness, as these kids morph from squirrelly, insecure freshman into calm, self-assured seniors, are astounding. And by the end of four years, I am as protective and proud of them as if they were my own.

Make no mistake: I am a tough taskmaster. I have extremely high expectations for these kids, as writers and as representatives of this publication. I give them an enormous amount of responsibility—and an enormous amount of freedom. They have press passes that allow them to move freely through the building during fifth hour as they gather the news and photos necessary to create a publication for their peers.

It thrills me to watch them rise to the occasion. In spite of their grumbling about tight deadlines and exhaustive rewrites, they consistently do better than they think they can.

What makes this class, and others like it, so satisfying is the fact that we are all working toward a common goal. In this class, students do not memorize facts to regurgitate on a test. They are using, in a profoundly practical way, every skill they were taught in Beginning Journalism. And as their skill base expands over time, their level of mastery deepens.

I know these kids are learning. I see it as they tackle increasingly challenging topics, or analyze their work for truth, fairness, and accuracy. They've become better interviewers. They've learned to ask hard questions, and to see several sides of an issue. They've learned (grudgingly) that deadlines are nonnegotiable. They've learned accountability and teamwork, because if they don't do their part the entire issue is compromised. They've become keenly aware of their responsibility to each other, and to our shared goal.

They are exuberantly engaged in the learning process.

To see them take the skills I taught them and put them to practical use is gratifying beyond belief. More importantly, when they leave this class, the skills they learned here, including unmeasured things like time management, professionalism, and courtesy, will serve them well for a lifetime.

Some of them go on to have careers in publishing. Melodee founded an alternative newspaper in Flint, Michigan. Brandon received an MFA from San Diego State University and teaches writing at the college level. Kirstie started a local magazine. But even the students who do not end up in publishing leave this class with an arsenal of skills that will be valuable in whatever career they choose.

A teaching experience like this is a blast, a blessing, sheer bliss for a teacher. This is authentic learning, with a practical application that allows us to show off what we've learned. Every time we distribute the paper to our community, we are so darn proud we could burst. Not only do these students earn class credit, a letter grade, and regular feedback from me, but they receive feedback from the community as well. We use this, too, and discuss the strengths and weaknesses of each issue after publication.

This classroom is a hub of happy activity. These kids, and this newspaper, are my pride and joy.

Sadly, this kind of teaching and learning experience has been squeezed out by an obsession with standardized testing. Today, everything that happens in the classroom boils down to The Test. Public education has been hijacked by big business and its propaganda machine, which works night and day to convince the public that standardized tests are the only way to measure learning. And because government funding is increasingly tied to those test scores and those test scores are tied to teacher pay, teachers are being forced by the government to teach in ways that go against their own best practices. They are forced to teach to the test.

Corporate reformers, billionaires, and the politicians indebted to them have worked hard to convince the general public that public schools are failing because teachers are lazy and incompetent. The media, fed by private interest groups and politicians with an agenda, have painted a picture of teachers, and the schools they teach in, as slovenly, unqualified, ill-equipped, and self-serving. They imply that there's a better way to teach, and an easier way to learn, but for some bizarre reason our nation's teachers choose to ignore it.

Hogwash.

Every teacher I know is well versed in a wide range of teaching strategies, such as differentiated instruction, collaborative inquiry, learning styles, and multiple intelligences. They are skilled at generating discovery and guiding students to make inferences and connections between what they read and what they've experienced. Long before the Common Core standards were introduced schools all across the country had excellent curricula in place and teachers synced their lessons with state standards and benchmarks.

But corporate reformers would have you believe that they have a better way, and that they are privy to some knowledge or strategy that veteran teachers are not.

Hooey.

The people taking the lead in education reform are not interested in what teachers have to say. Legislators continue to make decisions about education policy without input from the true experts in teaching and learning. "Studies" and "reports" that come out of so-called "think tanks" are given more credence than highly educated veteran teachers in real classrooms.

At first blush, to someone not well versed in current education reform, this seems nonsensical. Why wouldn't policy makers seek input from teachers? Why wouldn't teachers, the ones holding degrees in education and standing in front of students all day, be front and center in the education reform conversation?

Teachers are not included in the education reform conversation because, in reality, it has nothing to do with teaching and learning. For corporate reformers the goal is not, as they claim, global competitiveness or better educated students. They are not dismantling the public school system for altruistic reasons. For corporate reformers the bottom line is money. Every initiative they promote—Common Core standards, scripted lessons, virtual schools, charter schools, school choice, vouchers, standardized testing, tying teacher pay to student test scores—is ultimately about busting the teacher's union and dismantling the public school system.

The goal is privatization.

In many districts food, transportation, substitute teachers, and custodial services have already been privatized. If corporate reformers get their way and privatize schools completely, the bottom line will be profit, not learning. And without local oversight and open meetings, big business will be free to cut all kinds of corners to ensure large profits. They will not be accountable to the public. In a free market system, competition will rule. Privatized schools will need to compete for students, and they will do that by touting high test scores. And one way to keep those test scores high will be to deny access to any student who might bring them down.

Teaching jobs will go to the lowest bidder, not the best teacher. To keep costs down labor rights will be abolished and teachers will be paid less. Who will want a teaching job then? It won't be the best and the brightest, that's for sure.

While veteran teachers with thirty years experience and three degrees are being told they are not qualified under the No Child Left Behind Act, corporate reformers hail Teach for America recruits—kids right out of college who do NOT major in education but simply attend a five-week teaching boot camp—as education's saviors. Why? Because they would like you to believe that teaching is a job anyone can do.

It's illogical. If the goal of corporate reformers is truly to improve learning, why would they work to enact legislation that ties teacher pay to test scores, and then turn around and lower the requirements for new teachers?

The public, unprivatized school system is worth fighting for. It is fundamental to a democratic society. This richly diverse system serves everyone, regardless of race, religion, ability, or social class. Tuition free and publicly governed, public schools allow decision making at the community level. Neighborhood schools serve their communities and provide students with far more than an education: meals, transportation, health screening, before- and after-school programs, counseling, clothing, even glasses, not to mention lessons in socialization and what it means to be human.

The challenge of teaching and learning, and the struggles described in this book, are not idiosyncratic of the public school system. They're human struggles that can't be solved by charter schools, private schools, vouchers, or more testing.

Most importantly, our students are worth fighting for. Children need to be recognized for the beautifully unique beings they are, not stuffed into a one-size-fits-all mold. Children need to be allowed to fail, because through failure, they learn. School should be the place where children discover their purpose.

And that purpose is not to pass a test.

Standing in the buffet line at a Fourth of July barbecue, an acquaintance said to me, "I used to read the newspaper and wonder what in the world was going on in the public schools. I just couldn't figure out what had gone so wrong. It sounded like they were in shambles. Then I got a job in the public school system, and I see now that public schools are persecuted. Teachers are persecuted. I've never seen such hard-working people, such dedication in the face of such challenges. And for some reason, the public, and the media, just persecute them."

When she said that I thought about our district's curriculum meetings. Once a month the room is packed with teachers who come—voluntarily—to sit through a long, boring meeting after a full day of teaching.

Their feet hurt, their voices are tired, their backs ache. They are not required to be here. They do not get paid for it. They are here because they care about the curriculum. They care whether or not the children learn Step A before they are taught Step B. It *matters* to them. Their families wait supper at home, yet they sit through a three-hour meeting because they care.

These people are my heroes.

Still, as much as I love this teaching experience, I can't ignore the destructive changes being forced on my colleagues and me. I feel as if I am no longer a teacher, but rather a clerk, processing students instead of inspiring them. I am worn down by regulations and paperwork. As Nancy Carlsson-Paige said in the Foreword, "the business values of competition and measurement that are imposed on today's schools are all wrong for this vibrant place."

So, with equal parts bittersweet affection for my students, and a growing impatience with the inane initiatives of policymakers hell-bent on destroying public education, I left the classroom.

And now I tell the stories.

I tell the stories because my heart is still there, in that classroom. I tell the stories because current teachers are too overworked to do it. I tell the stories because teachers are too demoralized to do it.

I tell the stories because they are *important.*

Because they matter.

And because teachers need to know they're not alone.

I tell the stories because the public school system is worth saving.

The future of our students, our teachers, and indeed our nation, depends on it.

About the Author

Kelly Flynn is an education writer, speaker, public school advocate, and newspaper columnist whose commentary ran in *The Flint Journal* and the *Jackson Citizen Patriot*. She taught high school in Flint, Michigan, for nearly twenty years.